REALIZING THE

ANOINTING

OSEI NTI

Table of Contents

BACKGROUND OF THE ANOINTING

God's Anointing for Favor Throughout History. Throughout Bible times and continuing today, every stream of the anointing for favor is activated by faith! It was that anointing of favor in the Old Testament that caused Abram, later called Abraham, to prosper wherever he went, even as he obeyed God's voice and left his homeland to journey into the land of Canaan with at least 400 people who worked for him (Genesis 12). How was that possible? It was God's favor! His son Isaac was blessed when he sowed seed even in the midst of a great famine.

The harvest was so great that even the Philistine king, Abimelech, envied him (Genesis 26). People all around Isaac remained ruined by the drought, yet he was anointed with God's favor! Even in times of disaster, God's favor works for you, a believer, but not for your unbelieving neighbor. What caused Pharaoh's blessing and trust in an unknown young man named Joseph (Genesis 41) to the point that the imprisoned Hebrew was suddenly promoted to second-in-command over all Egypt?

Only God's anointing of favor can cause that! Generations later, why would another pharaoh give favor to Israel one fateful night when it was impossible to be favored? The Egyptians had been devastated by plagues, famine, and the loss of their firstborn male children. Who would ever imagine that the Israelites, coming to those decimated Egyptian homes in the middle of the night and asking for gifts, would be given so much that they left Egypt "spoiled" (meaning the land was stripped of its most valuable possessions and assets)

The children of Israel did according to the word of Moses; and they borrowed of the Egyptians jewels of silver, and jewels of gold, and raiment: And the Lord gave the people favour in the sight of the Egyptians, so that they lent unto them such things as they required. And they spoiled the Egyptians. (Exodus 12:35-36 The wealth of Egypt was literally poured out on the Israelites, and all their needs were met because of the incredible power of the favor anointing. We know that the journey from Egypt to the Promised Land should have taken 11 days, but because of a lack of trust and faith, it ended up taking 40 years.

But even then, God made sure the children of Israel were cared for, not only keeping their clothing and shoes from wearing out (Deuteronomy 29:5 L), but keeping their livestock, numbering in the millions, well-fed and cared for. How was that possible? Millions of their cattle, sheep, and other livestock wandered through the desert and received water and food, yet the Israelites didn't own any water rights or grow any crops. The Israelites obviously left Egypt with so much spoil that their provisions lasted the entire 40 years! Only the favor of God could do that, and that is the anointing I'm talking about! It was that anointing that sustained Job, even when he lost virtually everything through unspeakable reversals and tragedies. In the end, however, the anointing for favor caused the Lord to bless Job's obedience and faith with "twice as much as he had before" (Job 42:10 L).

David, though his enemies tried to destroy him, fought against the Amalekites at Ziklag and recovered all--with so much spoil that he even sent gifts to all the thousands of elders of Judah. These weren't small tokens; they were substantial gifts delivered to each one (1 Samuel 30). And it was that anointing for favor on the life of Solomon that caused the world to honor him with gold, silver, and jewels beyond description (2 Chronicles 1-10)! That anointing continued into New Testament times.

Favor was clearly evident upon Jesus Christ and the apostles. It was this same anointing that we read about when Peter preached to the church to go sell their land and properties and bring the money to the church: All that believed were together, and had all things common; and sold their possessions and goods, and parted them to all men, as every man had need.

And they, continuing daily with one accord in the temple, and breaking bread from house to house, did eat their meat with gladness and singleness of heart, praising God, and having favour with all the people. And the Lord added to the church daily such as should be saved. (Acts 2:44-47 L)

What would move thousands of people to listen to Peter, then become believers and givers? Only the anointing for favor could do that. Moses talked about the anointing for favor in relation to biblical abundance:

"All these blessings shall come on thee, and overtake thee, if thou shalt hearken unto the voice of the LORD thy God. Blessed shalt thou be in the city, and blessed shalt thou be in the field" (Deuteronomy 28:2-3 L).And it was also that anointing for favor mentioned in verse 12: "The Lord shall open unto thee his good treasure, the heaven to give the rain unto thy land in his season, and to bless all the work of thine hand." Only the anointing for favor can accomplish these things for a nation, a family, or an individual!

ACTIVATING GOD'S ANOINTING FOR FAVOR

Notice this: Throughout Scripture, the anointing for favor was activated by faith. Favor is a gift of God to His people, and it is only given to the obedient--those who are givers. All the people and groups I've mentioned were givers. Abraham gave to Melchizedek, and even greater favor was released on him. Favor was released on Isaac when he gave God an offering. Favor was released on the nation of Israel when they offered a lamb in every household.

Jesus spoke often about giving, and the anointing for favor was upon the apostles, as our Lord Jesus taught:Give, and it shall be given unto you; good measure, pressed down, and shaken together, and running over shall men give into your bosom. For with the same measure that ye mete withal it shall be measured to you again. (Luke 6:38 L)

Notice the reference to "men give into your bosom." In Scripture, the reference to bosom refers to a "place of comfort," so that literally means that men (the people and circumstances that surround you) will give and add blessings that pertain to the peace and comfort of your own life and that of your family. So why would a man give you anything unless God had placed an anointing on your life?

It is the power of that blessed anointing! Dear partner, I believe this anointing belongs to you as a child of God! It is your covenant right to have it every day. But it's the act of giving that releases the treasures of heaven on your life and triggers the anointing for God's favor and blessing. If you want favor on your home, your job, your family situations, even opportunities and inheritances that will arise in 2014, you must begin planting now.

Harvest and favor always follow seed-time. Without planting, there is no harvest! A spiritual miracle demands a spiritual act, while a physical miracle demands a physical act, and a financial miracle demands a financial act. When someone is saved they must confess Christ publicly. When someone is healed, they must step out in faith. And you cannot prosper financially unless you act in faith as you give to God's work. That is how the anointing for favor is released.

That is the order of Scripture. It is impossible to prosper under the anointing without an act of faith, and it is impossible without an act of faith occurring and reoccurring continually in your life. Miracles happen when we give God something to work with. And when we sow seed into His kingdom, we release our faith so God can use what we give for His glory and the favor He gives! I truly believe that 2014 will be a year when we see a powerful anointing for favor among believers who understand this principle and act on it.

So today, I feel strongly in my spirit that I need to do something for you that you must experience. I am providing a special prayer form on which you can list your most urgent needs for me to pray over. Remember, every stream of favor is released by faith!The Day of Prayer for God's Anointing of Favor.My heart is truly exploding with faith for you, and in late December I will pray for your most urgent needs, especially your financial ones, during the Day of Prayer for God's Anointing of Favor.

It will be a powerful, anointed time of intercession! As I enter my 40th year of ministry this month--a ministry bathed in prayer throughout the years--God is directing me to focus even more on prayer. I know that 2014 is going to be a breakthrough year for new heights of intercession and prayer. All seven of our ministry offices around the world and our Mighty Warriors Prayer Army are gearing up for an even greater focus on prayer.

And I'm calling all of our staff members, prayer warriors, and my partners to join in agreement for you during our Day of Prayer for God's Anointing of Favor! There is nothing supernatural about a paper form or a drop of oil...that is, until God steps in. Jesus assures us that when you and I agree "as touching any thing they shall ask, it shall be done for them" (Matthew 18:19 L).

What an amazing promise! I encourage you to take a step of faith by giving your best seed-gift along with submitting your prayer needs. God desires for us to move into a new anointing for His favor in 2014! And I want to do whatever I can to encourage you to claim the promises available to you as a covenant believer.

You must increase your seed level to increase your harvest level, because that's what releases the anointing for favor. Every level of giving releases your faith. You must release greater seed in order to release a greater harvest. It is impossible to see a greater harvest if you are content to give sparingly! You have to move to new levels of seed.

So if you've been giving $20 a month toward the Gospel, give $40 and see what happens. If you've been giving $40, move up to a higher level, perhaps $80. If $50, then $100. Double your seed for an even greater harvest, as greater faith releases the anointing for favor in your life! If you have been at a low-level harvest for a long time, then it's time to release God's favor with higher seed-level giving. It's time to move into a higher dimension of faith as you release this anointing over yourself and your loved ones! Be courageous today.

Be bold. Step into your covenant position and favor. Secure your financial tomorrow by acting today! As a step of faith, give your most generous seed-gift. Be sure to include your requests for our Day of Prayer for God's Anointing of Favor. I look forward to hearing from you and anointing your prayer request list with oil, then sending it back to you. Love you always and thank you for being my sweetest .

ANOINTING

A distinction was made by the ancient Hebrews between anointing with oil in private use, as in making one's toilet (cukh), and anointing as a religious rite (mashach)

1. Ordinary Use:

(1) As regards its secular or ordinary use, the native olive oil, alone or mixed with perfumes, was commonly used for toilet purposes, the very poor naturally reserving it for special occasions only (Ruth 3:3). The fierce protracted heat and biting lime dust of Palestine made the oil very soothing to the skin, and it was applied freely to exposed parts of the body, especially to the face (Psalms 104:15).

(2) The practice was in vogue before David's time, and traces of it may be found throughout the Old Testament (see Deuteronomy 28:40; Ruth 3:3; 2 Samuel 12:20; 14:2; 2 Chron 28:15; Ezekiel 16:9; Micah 6:15; Daniel 10:3) and in the New Testament (Matthew 6:17, etc.). Indeed it seems to have been a part of the daily toilet throughout the East.

(3) To abstain from it was one token of mourning (2 Samuel 14:2; compare Matthew 6:17), and to resume it a sign that the mourning was ended (2 Samuel 12:20; 14:2; Daniel 10:3; Judith 10:3). It often accompanied the bath (Ruth 3:3; 2 Samuel 12:20; Ezekiel 16:9; Susanna 17), and was a customary part of the preparation for a feast (Ecclesiastes 9:8; Psalms 23:5). One way of showing honor to a guest was to anoint his head with oil (Psalms 23:5; Luke 7:46); a rarer and more striking way was to anoint his feet (Luke 7:38). In James 5:14, we have an instance of anointing with oil for medicinal purposes, for which see OIL.

2. Religious Use:

Anointing as a religious rite was practiced throughout the ancient East in application both to persons and to things.

(1) It was observed in Canaan long before the Hebrew conquest, and, accordingly, Weinel (Stade's Zeutschrift, XVIII, 50) holds that, as the use of oil for general purposes in Israel was an agricultural custom borrowed from the Canaanites, so the anointing with sacred oil was an outgrowth from its regular use for toilet purposes. It seems more in accordance with the known facts of the case and the terms used in description to accept the view set forth by Robertson Smith (Religion of the Semites, 2nd ed., 233, 383; compare Wellhausen, Reste des arabischen Heidenthums, 2nd ed., 125) and to believe that the cukh or use of oil for toilet purposes, was of agricultural and secular origin, and that the use of oil for sacred purposes, mashach, was in origin nomadic and sacrificial. Robertson Smith finds the origin of the sacred anointing in the very ancient custom of smearing the sacred fat on the altar (matstsebhah), and claims, rightly it would seem, that from the first there was a distinct and consistent usage, distinguishing the two terms as above.

(2) The primary meaning of mashach in Hebrew, which is borne out by the Arabic, seems to have been "to daub" or "smear." It is used of painting a ceiling in Jeremiah 22:14, of anointing a shield in Isaiah 21:5, and is, accordingly, consistently applied to sacred furniture, like the altar, in Exodus 29:36 and Daniel 9:24, and to the sacred pillar in Genesis 31:13:"where thou anointedst a pillar."

(3) The most significant uses of mashach, however, are found in its application, not to sacred things, but to certain sacred persons. The oldest and most sacred of these, it would seem, was the anointing of the king, by pouring oil upon his head at his coronation, a ceremony regarded as sacred from the earliest times, and observed religiously not in Israel only, but in Egypt and elsewhere (see Judges 9:8,15; 1 Samuel 9:16; 10:1;2 Samuel 19:10; 1 Kings 1:39,45; 2 Kings 9:3,6; 11:12). Indeed such anointing appears to have been reserved exclusively for the king in the earliest times, which accounts for the fact that "the Lord's anointed" became a synonym for "king" (see 1 Samuel 12:3,5; 26:11; 2 Samuel 1:14; Psalms 20:6). It is thought by some that the practice originated in Egypt, and it is known to have been observed as a rite in Canaan at a very early day. Tell el-Amarna Letters 37 records the anointing of a king.

(4) Among the Hebrews it was believed not only that it effected a transference to the anointed one of something of the holiness and virtue of the deity in whose name and by whose representative the rite was performed, but also that it imparted a special endowment of the spirit of Yahweh (compare 1 Samuel 16:13; Isaiah 61:1). Hence the profound reverence for the king as a sacred personage, "the anointed" (Hebrew, meshiach YHWH), which passed over into our language through the Greek Christos, and appears as "Christ
".

(5) In what is known today as the Priestly Code, the high priest is spoken of as "anointed" (Exodus 29:7; Leviticus 4:3; 8:12), and, in passages

regarded by some as later additions to the Priestly Code, other priests also are thus spoken of (Exodus 30:30; 40:13-15). Elijah was told to anoint Elisha as a prophet (1 Kings 19:16), but seems never to have done so. 1 Kings 19:16 gives us the only recorded instance of such a thing as the anointing of a prophet. Isaiah 61:1 is purely metaphorical (compare Dillmann on Leviticus 8:12-14 with ICC on Numbers 3:3; see also Nowack, Lehrbuch der hebraischen Archaologie, II, 124).

5 SIGNS OF AN ANOINTED LEADER

In 1 Samuel 10 Saul is anointed as King over Israel. As soon as he was anointed as the leader 5 signs occurred that I see in the leaders of today, or I should say the great anointed leaders of today.

New Heart (9). God changed everything about him. His new heart gave him the compassion, the passion & determination to lead. He had a new found ability to control his emotions and thoughts in ways he never knew before. A new heart from God, brings new priorities & paths.

New Words (10). He prophesied with the prophets. He spoke about the things & plans of God with boldness and great conviction. This is certainly the characteristic of an anointed leader! He hears from God, and proclaims it with boldness. Not walking in fear of man, but in reverent fear of God!

New Followers (26). "Valiant" men immediately were called by God to go to his side. When you are an anointed leader, God will always send valiant men & women to surround you and hold up your arms. They will guard you, speak life into you, and also the truth-even if it hurts.

New Enemies (27). When you are truly an anointed leader, the vision God whispers in your ear and those words you hear from God and proclaim, will draw critics and enemies out of the wood work! Don't be caught off guard. Great leaders have great enemies!

New Authority (7). "Do whatever the occasion requires, for God is with you." God raises up great leaders for great purposes. When they begin to put everything in place to fulfill that great purpose, many decisions will have to be made. Great leaders show humility, honor & confidence in decision making. Those following them trust them, because they can see God's anointing on their lives.Â They know they hear from God, and are determined to do what God says, and only what God says!

So, the question should be: If you are a leader do you have all of these signs? If you don't, maybe God hasn't brought you to your full place of leadership yet. Be patient, you can't rush the process! Saul lost his anointing for being impatient

1) PREACHING ANOINTING

You can go to a teaching, he can shout but there's no change in your life. Preaching without the anointing is the same as a motivational speaker. There must be an anointing in that man's life for it to penetrate your life. The anointing must be on the preacher's life and on his ministry. You cannot forget an anointed sermon. The preaching anointing change lives!

2) TEACHING ANOINTING

Jesus taught the Beattitudes, teaching not preaching. The anointing of God in the life of Christ caused the people to be so attentive, the people said 'he speaks with such authority.' He got the attention of the crowds. The same with Peter in the day of Pentecost. Preaching moves the life of a sinner. Peter preached and sinners heard. In Acts 15 when they gathered in Jerusalem, Peter taught. Peter was preaching in the house of Cornelious but was teaching in Jerusalem when sharing the testimony of what happened in the house of Cornelious.

A teaching anointing will fill the heart. A preaching anointing will stir the heart. Anointing stirs anointing. Bible scriptures were crystal clear. Without the anointing we cannot be fed.

3) HEALING ANOINTING

This anointing it's completely different. You can sense the change in the atmosphere. Why? It drives away demons and disease. You can preach the gospel but that anointing will not drive away demons. You can teach and that anointing cannot drive away demons or disease.

ISimon the sorcerer was delivered but not healed. The healing anointing will still not drive away demons. It will drive away sickness. There are different groups of demons. Jesus said 'this kind.' Some are driven away by the healing anointing. The majority are driven away by the deliverance anointing.The healing anointing, even though all anointings are equal, is not the same as the deliverance anointing. Jesus sent the 12 then the 70 with anointing oil. Healings can take place when the simplest Christians pray but deliverance from demons is a different thing. Healing the sick, that anointing comes on you, it comes as we surrender.

14

4) DELIVERANCE ANOINTING

Roaring anointing, sets captives free. It's not an easy anointing. It's a rough anointing. It's like a mighty wind. It requires a punch from heaven.The healing anointing is gentle. I have never known a deliverance anointing so gentle. You cannot cast out demons by just saying – come out. Everything in you becomes violent, focused.
I can be gentle when I speak to someone be healed. You don't see Jesus speaking softly when casting out demons.

5) PROPHETIC/REVELATION ANOINTING

When you're reading the Bible so you can understand the Word. You can give a prophetic word of knowledge or wisdom to others (1 Co. 14:3) and be part of a prophetic ministry.

6) WORSHIP ANOINTING

This kind of anointing it's connected to praise. Worshipping God, praising God. It's so powerful when you get in the Spirit.

7) PROSPERITY ANOINTING

This kind of anointing it's mentioned in many Scriptures.Deut 8:18 - God has the power to get wealth.Deut 28:12 and on – you can work until your hands bleed and you won't be prosperous. God is the one who blesses the work of your hand. You can't be overtaken by blessings unless there's favor on your life. Men will respond to you because of the anointing. Joseph had the anointing. The anointing to prosper and to be promoted is the same anointing. The same anointing that come on the Hebrews who went to the Egyptians homes at midnight to ask for their wealth.

3 million people with favor. The chance of every Egyptian saying yes? May 1, 2 or 3 will say yes, but the whole nation? You cannot have such favor unless God is in it. Favor is the anointing for prosperity.If God gave the Jewish people favor in the sight of their enemies how much more will He give you?What would cause Solomon to get money from just speaking? They brought him gold by the ship load. The bible doesn't say he bought. His servants went and got the gold. What would cause the nations to give Solomon gold? Favor – the anointing for prosperity.

That anointing will keep you alive, will keep your boss liking you, will keep you out of debt. Giving releases the anointing for prosperity.

Many persons do not really know much about what the Bible says about the Holy Spirit. If you personally do want to have an increase of people in your church, or more love, joy, faith, in your own life, and to be able to resist the continual onslaughts of the enemy the devil you need to be now anointed with the Holy Spirit and you need to get to know him and his works better too.

Generally the works of the Holy spirit have an initial beginning but they are also continual works, evolving ones. God is complex and so is the work of the holy spirit as well.. 7 is the number of spiritual perfection.. to be perfect we should experience all of God 7 anointing now too..

PERSONALITY OR NATURE

The Holy Spirit is a person who combines the 7 Spirits of God, **EXPRESSIONS OF GOD'S CHARACTER,** (Isa 11:2 KJV) And the spirit of the LORD shall rest upon him, the spirit of wisdom and understanding, the spirit of counsel and might, the spirit of knowledge and of the fear of the LORD;Isaiah 11:2 And the spirit of the LORD shall rest upon him,

the spirit of wisdom

and understanding,

the spirit of counsel

and might,

the spirit of knowledge

and of the fear of the LORD;

with righteousness shall he judge

– 3 And shall make him of quick understanding in the fear of the LORD: and he shall not judge after the sight of his eyes, neither reprove after the hearing of his ears: 4 But with righteousness shall he judge the poor, and reprove with equity for the meek of the earth: and he shall smite the earth: with the rod of his mouth, and with the breath of his lips shall he slay the wicked.

Proverbs 8:12 I wisdom dwell with prudence, and find out knowledge of witty inventions. 13 The fear of the LORD is to hate evil: pride, and arrogance, and the evil way, and the froward mouth, do I hate. 14 Counsel is mine, and sound wisdom: I am understanding; I have strength. 15 By me kings reign, and princes decree justice. 16 By me princes rule, and nobles, even all the judges of the earth.

AGAIN THE SEVEN SPIRITUAL ATTRIBUTES OR ANOINTINGS THAT EXPRESS THE CHARACTER OF GOD

– Spirit of Weeping and Sorrow, Holy Spirit Travail, Anointings,
-Holiness the Spirit of Holiness
-The Spirit of Mercy and Compassion,
-Joy or Rejoicing
-Spirit of Zeal
-Spirit of Power
-Spirit of Wisdom and Truth.

1 GOD'S SPIRIT OF SORROW

is at the center of intercession. It is travailing sorrow that results in the fruit of deliverance. It is the Spiritual device God uses in the supernatural breaking of yokes. The anointing takes upon itself a focus persons who are lost, in a great need or those who are bound.Christ is ever touched by the feeling of our weakness or infirmities!

The anointing of The Lord's sorrow is transferred to intercessors who travail for those who have been taken prey by spiritual enemies. While

Jesus has and is come to seek and to save those who are lost, the Devil has come and will continue to come, to steal, kill, and destroy. Sorrow as an anointing is manifested by the Spirit giving voice to groaning and deep anguish beyond words.

Tears of Godly sorrow brings forth repentance after it has had enough time to complete the Holy Spirit's work. The breaking and release is signaled by an outrushing of joy or laughter.One who is yielded to this Spirit of God begins to lament and be sorrowful as the Holy Spirit begins to initiate this anointing within. It can be faked or counterfeited, but then its power and usefulness are lost.

Any such act of the flesh produces no fruit.Though observable, deep anointings of intercession can not be learned.The anointing of Godly sorrow supersedes all personal cares and feelings. However, The Spirit of God will use personal sorrow as a starting point and turn it into Godly sorrow. Personal sorrow is directed self-ward,

but Godly sorrow other-ward. Godly intercession interacts with several anointings; sorrow, joy, warring anger, praise and worship, according to the moving of the Spirit.At the point of release spiritual sorrow will normally always end with joy and laughter.Scriptural References to the Sorrow of God   "Jesus wept." (-- John 11:35) >

"For godly sorrow worketh repentance to salvation not to be repented of: but the sorrow of the world worketh death."(-- 2 Corinthians 7:10) "Who hath heard such a thing? who hath seen such things? Shall the earth be made to bring forth in one day? or shall a nation be born at once? for as soon as Zion travailed, she brought forth her children." (-- Isaiah 66:8)

"My little children, of whom I travail in birth again until Christ be formed in you," (-- Galatians 4:19) "And at the evening sacrifice I arose up from my heaviness; and having rent my garment and my mantle, I fell upon my knees, and spread out my hands unto the LORD my God,"(– Ezra 9:5) "Depart from me, all ye workers of iniquity; for the LORD hath heard the voice of my weeping." (-- Psalms 6:8)

"The LORD hath heard my supplication; the LORD will receive my prayer." (-- Psalms 6:9) "For his anger endureth but a moment; in his favour is life: weeping may endure for a night, but joy cometh in the morning."(-- Psalms 30:5) "And in that day did the Lord GOD of hosts call to weeping, and to mourning, and to baldness, and to girding with sackcloth:"(-- Isaiah 22:12)

"They shall come with weeping, and with supplications will I lead them: I will cause them to walk by the rivers of waters in a straight way, wherein they shall not stumble:" (-- Jeremiah 31:9) "That I have great heaviness and continual sorrow in my heart." (– Romans 9:2) "And he (Jesus) took with him Peter and the two sons of Zebedee, and began to be sorrowful and very heavy." (-- Matthew 26:37)

"And when he was come near, he beheld the city, and wept over it," (-- Luke 19:41) "Blessed are ye that hunger now: for ye shall be filled. Blessed are ye that weep now: for ye shall laugh."(-- Luke 6:21) "Rejoice with them that do rejoice, and weep with them that weep." (-- Romans 12:15)

"Verily, verily, I say unto you, That ye shall weep and lament, but the world shall rejoice: and ye shall be sorrowful, but your sorrow shall be turned into joy."(-- John 16:20)

"A woman when she is in travail hath sorrow, because her hour is come: but as soon as she is delivered of the child, she remembereth no more the anguish, for joy that a man is born into the world."(-- John 16:21)

"For I have heard a voice as of a woman in travail, and the anguish as of her that bringeth forth her first child, the voice of the daughter of Zion, that bewaileth herself, that spreadeth her hands, saying, Woe is me now! for my soul is wearied because of murderers."(-- Jeremiah 4:31)

"For we know that the whole creation groaneth and travaileth in pain together until now."(-- Romans 8:22) "And not only they, but ourselves also, which have the first fruits of the Spirit, even we ourselves groan within ourselves, waiting for the adoption, to wit, the redemption of our body."(-- Romans 8:23)

2 THE SPIRIT OF HOLINESS: (WORSHIP AND HOLY FEAR)

Though there are numerous listings of the Spirit of Holiness it is hard to account it strictly as an anointing.Where other anointings find expression in action and word, the spirit of Holiness finds expression in inaction and awed reverence. The closer we come to experiencing God face to face the more this power is revealed. God is Holy and so far above all that is human and mundane to be indescribable.

The human 'son of man' who finds himself or herself in the proximity of God becomes as "one who is dead".   In this state we do not think, we do not speak, we do not carry on with any of the normal human senses, we are incapacitated toward any action but fear and awe. God only releases us to return to the world of flesh and material limitations.

True Worship is encompassed by the Spirit of Holiness. There is little that any created or begotten creature can do in the manifested presence of God other than to fall before him in total "awe-full" submission.

The Spirit of Holiness provides understanding to the phrase "fear of the Lord." Encounters with the Lord as depicted by Ezekiel, Isaiah, John and others describe the son of man falling as dead in His presence, in the Holy of Holies His awesome power is manifested; no priest can stand to minister; the angels cry 'holy'.

The elders and patriots bow in surrender the earth trembles before him; every living thing waits breathlessly before Him in silence. The anointings of God are awaiting believers who desire to move deeper in God.

Today many in Christian churches make no separation between the psychological realm of the mind and thought, and the spiritual.

It is the power of God that fuels the spiritual while human abilities fuel the efforts of the natural man. Experiencing the Word of God in power is what the apostle's doctrine urges. God desires to manifest His virtue, thought, and powers through earthen vessels so that the excellence of manifestation may be attributed to God and not man.

The power of God through the Holy Spirit makes the experience of God's Holy presence a reality and supplies the child of God with a taste of that which is entirely from God. No eye has seen nor hear has heard what God has prepared for those who love Him. But now it is revealed by the Holy Spirit.- – 1Corinthians 2:9

3: THE SPIRIT OF COMPASSION:

The Spirit of Adoption
(The Tender Mercies of God the Father).For the Lord is Good and His Mercies endure forever! The Goodness of God is the source of all grace and blessing.

The Father's heart of forgiveness and compassion are revealed again and again throughout scripture and are at the center of all Jesus' ministry. Mercy, compassion, forgiveness; Mercy, compassion, healing; Mercy, compassion, restoration; Mercy, compassion, deliverance. The mercies of God directed to weak and fallible souls is the greatest wonder of the universe!

The simplicity of the phrase "tender mercies" reflects so powerfully the kindness of God, the Good Shepherd who cares for and nurtures his flock.

The same father who receives the prodigal and clothes him with a fine robe and prepares the fatted calf for feasting, fills our own cup to overflowing!The kindness of God is expressed in the ministering hand a friend and comforter.

Agape love is the love which expresses itself in gestures of kindness, in actions of giving compassion.It is the heart of Jesus' ministry when He declares, "the Son of Man came not to be ministered to by to minister." Ministery in the Greek word source means simply to serve

."How excellent is thy lovingkindness, O God! therefore the children of men put their trust under the shadow of thy wings." (– Psalms 36:7)"Yet the LORD will command his lovingkindness in the daytime, and in the

night his song shall be with me, and my prayer unto the God of my life."
(-- Psalms 42:8)."To the chief Musician,

A Psalm of David, when Nathan the prophet came unto him, after He had gone in to Bathsheba. Have mercy upon me, O God, according to thy lovingkindness: according unto the multitude of thy tender mercies blot out my transgressions." (-- Psalms 51:1)"

Because thy lovingkindness is better than life, my lips shall praise thee." (– Psalms 63:3)."Withhold not thou thy tender mercies from me, O LORD: let thy lovingkindness and thy truth continually preserve me." -- Psalms 40:11."Who redeemeth thy life from destruction; who crowneth thee with lovingkindness and tender mercies;" (-- Psalms 103:4)."Let thy tender mercies come unto me, that I may live: for thy law is my delight." (-- Psalms 119:77)."

The LORD is good to all: and his tender mercies are over all his works." (– Psalms 145:9)."But though he cause grief, yet will he have compassion according to the multitude of his mercies."(– Lamentations 3:32)."

He will turn again, he will have compassion upon us; he will subdue our iniquities; and thou wilt cast all their sins into the depths of the sea." (-- Micah 7:19)"But when he saw the multitudes, he was moved with compassion on them, because they fainted, and were scattered abroad, as sheep having no shepherd." (-- Matthew 9:36)"And Jesus went forth, and saw a great multitude, and was moved with compassion toward them, and he healed their sick."

(– Matthew 14:14)"Shouldest not thou also have had compassion on thy fellow servant, even as I had pity on thee?" (– Matthew 18:33)"So Jesus had compassion on them, and touched their eyes: and immediately their eyes received sight, and they followed him

." (– Matthew 20:34)."But a certain Samaritan, as he journeyed, came where he was: and when he saw him, he had compassion on him," (-- Luke 10:33)"Finally, be ye all of one mind, having compassion one of another, love as brethren, be pitiful, be courteous:"

(– 1 Peter 3:8)."For if our heart condemn us, God is greater than our heart, and knoweth all things." (– 1 John 3:20)."And there came a leper to him, beseeching him, and kneeling down to him, and saying unto him, If thou wilt, thou canst make me clean." "And Jesus, moved with compassion, put forth his hand, and touched him, and saith unto him, I will; be thou clean." (-- Mark 1:40,41)

4: THE SPIRIT OF PRAISE AND REJOICING: (THE SPIRIT OF JOY)

I have found a surprising spiritual link between apparent opposites, sorrow and joy. The Holy Spirit turns mourning into dancing, heaviness into praise, weeping into rejoicing. There is an ultimate point in the cycle of the Holy Spirit's travail when tears of sorrow turn into victory and darkness turns into the breaking dawn of hope. Therefore joy and sorrow are bonded pairs and blend into one another.

Again, joy is not a human emotion on this level but an anointed expression of the Spirit. Thanksgiving and praise follow breakthroughs of the Spirit. Holy laughter though ridiculed by those who have not experienced it is part of the richness of the spiritual life. When we are anointed with the Spirit of Joy, a vast separation is manifested between the material and the spiritual world; cares and heaviness give way to confidence. We sense that God is our total victory and that He will never leave us nor forsake us.

Our hearts are lifted up to the high places where we all sit with Him in heavenly places!"Thou lovest righteousness, and hatest wickedness: therefore God, thy God, hath anointed thee with the oil of gladness above thy fellows."(– Psalms 45:7"To appoint unto them that mourn in Zion, to give unto them beauty for ashes, the oil of joy for mourning, the garment of praise for the spirit of heaviness; " (-- Isaiah 61:3)"So that the people could not discern the noise of the shout of joy from the noise of the weeping of the people: for the people shouted with a loud shout, and the noise was heard afar off."(-- Ezra 3:13)"Thou hast made known to me the ways of life; Thou shalt make me full of joy with thy countenance." (– Acts 2:28)"

Thou wilt show me the path of life: in thy presence is fulness of joy; at thy right hand there are pleasures for evermore."(-- Psalms 16:11)"Thou hast turned for me my mourning into dancing: Thou hast put off my sackcloth, and girded me with gladness;"(– Psalms 30:11)"And David danced before the LORD with all his might; and David was girded with a linen ephod." (-- 2 Samuel 6:14)

5: THE SPIRIT OF ZEAL   THE SPIRIT OF JUDGMENT: SPIRIT OF BURNING   (THE ZEAL OF GOD IS AS A CONSUMING FIRE)

The study of the "Zeal of God" encompasses the entire question of God's anger, wrath and judgment and those upon whom it is directed. In the time of the Old Covenant we see prophets and judges who exercised God's judgment against the unrighteous nations. These wicked nations served demon gods. Almighty God commanded their destruction.

After Jesus' ministry, the dispensation of the church age began and with church age the focus of this spirit of judgment has shifted. We no longer come against people who are wicked because of the Lord's example to forgive and bless those who do evil.

Yet we do see the Spirit of Judgment and zeal demonstrated by Jesus. It was however, directed against those in the world of religion who withstood the Spirit of God. The cleansing of the temple accounts reflects the zeal of God. We call this kind of anointing righteous anger.

Today our enemies are revealed to be spiritual and not in flesh. Today, prayers of imprecation (asking for vengeance and destruction of our enemies) as spoken by the prophets and psalmist are appropriate only if targeted to spiritual rulership in heavenly places and not against human beings."

When the Lord shall have washed away the filth of the daughters of Zion, and shall have purged the blood of Jerusalem from the midst thereof by the spirit of judgment, and by the spirit of burning." (-- Isaiah 4:4)"And for a spirit of judgment to him that sitteth in judgment, and for strength to them that turn the battle to the gate."(-- Isaiah 28:6)"But truly I am full of power by the spirit of the LORD, and of judgment, and of might, to declare unto Jacob his transgression, and to Israel his sin."(-- Micah 3:8)"

For the zeal of thine house hath eaten me up; and the reproaches of them that reproached thee are fallen upon me." (– Psalms 69:9)"Of the increase of his government and peace there shall be no end, upon the throne of David, and upon his kingdom, to order it, and to establish it with judgment and with justice from henceforth even for ever. The zeal of the LORD of hosts will perform this." (-- Isaiah 9:7)"My zeal hath consumed me, because mine enemies have forgotten thy words." (-- Psalms 119:139)

"Thus shall mine anger be accomplished, and I will cause my fury to rest upon them, and I will be comforted: and they shall know that I the LORD have spoken it in my zeal, when I have accomplished my fury in them." (-- Ezekiel 5:13)."When the Lord shall have washed away the filth of the daughters of Zion, and shall have purged the blood of Jerusalem from the midst thereof by the spirit of judgment, and by the spirit of burning."(– Isaiah 4:4)

6: THE ANOINTING OF POWER

DUNAMIS, doo'-nam-is; from G1410; force (lit. or fig.); spec. miraculous power (usually by impl. a miracle itself):–ability, abundance, meaning, might (-ily, -y, -y deed), (worker of) miracle (-s), power, strength, violence, mighty (wonderful) work._

The Anointing of Power.God is a God of Power and Might. By His word the worlds are created. By His word the creation stands. He commands life to be and it is. The greatness of God is fathomless. His power to us who believe is beyond comprehension. What is this powerful attribute of God which raised Jesus from the dead? What is the power which can create the miraculous? With a word He will call the sleeping dead to arise from their graves and will quicken mortal bodies.

Men of power were anointed in Strength:"And the spirit of the LORD came mightily upon him, and he rent him as he would have rent a kid, and he had nothing in his hand:." -- Judges 14:6"And the spirit of the LORD came upon him, and he went down to Ashkelon, and slew thirty men of them, and took their spoil, " -- Judges 14:19

28

"And when he came unto Lehi, the Philistines shouted against him: and the spirit of the LORD came mightily upon him, and the cords that were upon his arms became as flax that was burnt with fire, and his bands loosed from off his hands." (– Judges 15:14)"

But truly I am full of power by the spirit of the LORD, and of judgment, and of might, to declare unto Jacob his transgression, and to Israel his sin." (-- Micah 3:8)"Jesus saith unto him, Thou hast said: nevertheless I say unto you, Hereafter shall ye see the Son of man sitting on the right hand of power(dunamai),

and coming in the clouds of heaven." (– Matthew 26:64)"Now to him that is of power to establish you according to my Gospel, and the preaching of Jesus Christ, according to the revelation of the mystery, which was kept secret since the world began," (– Romans 16:25)"And my speech and my preaching was not with enticing words of man's wisdom, but in demonstration of the Spirit and of power:"(1 Corinthians 2:4)"Knowing that he which raised up the Lord Jesus shall raise up us also by Jesus, and shall present us with you."(2 Corinthians 4:14) That I might know Him in the power of His resurrection-" (Phillipians 3:10)

7: THE SPIRIT OF WISDOM AND UNDERSTANDING: (THE SPIRIT OF TRUTH)

To truly discern it is to know the mind and heart of God. To know the full reality. To have this heart within you, is a guiding light of wisdom and knowledge that at once, knows the truth. In this anointing we know that God is our Father; that the Bible is his divine voice speaking the word of truth; often that human voices written or spoken, are speaking from personal vanity or from divine revelation.The Lord Jesus announced to his disciples (Both his original and his current -- including our current generation, if we believe on His name) that he would send us a comforter, a teacher. Jesus refers to this helper as the Spirit of Truth.

It is this spirit of wisdom, truth, and understanding who is the voice of the witness, the Great Amen, the voice of the Good Shepherd in John 10: v 4. "And thou shalt speak unto all that are wise hearted, whom I have filled with the spirit of wisdom, that they may make Aaron's garments to consecrate him, that he may minister unto me in the priest's office." (-- Exodus 28:3)"

And I have filled him with the spirit of God, in wisdom, and in understanding, and in knowledge, and in all manner of workmanship," (- Exodus 31:3) "And I, behold, I have given with him Aholiab, the son of Ahisamach, of the tribe of Dan: and in the hearts of all that are wise hearted I have put wisdom, that they may make all that I have commanded thee;" (-- Exodus 31:6)"

And Joshua the son of Nun was full of the spirit of wisdom; for Moses had laid his hands upon him: and the children of Israel hearkened unto him, and did as the LORD commanded Moses." (- Deuteronomy 34:9) "And the spirit of the LORD shall rest upon him, the spirit of wisdom and understanding, the spirit of counsel and might, the spirit of knowledge and of the fear of the LORD;"(- Isaiah 11:2) "That the God of our Lord Jesus Christ, the Father of glory, may give unto you the spirit of wisdom and revelation in the knowledge of him:" (-- Ephesians 1:17)"

And I will pray the Father, and he shall give you another Comforter, that He may abide with you for ever;" (-- John 14:16) "Even the Spirit of truth; whom the world cannot receive, because it seeth him not, neither knoweth him: but ye know him; for he dwelleth with you, and shall be in you." (– John 14:17)"But when the Comforter is come, whom I will send unto you from the Father, even the Spirit of truth, which proceedeth from the Father, He shall testify of me:" -- John 15:26

1 **GOD'S SPIRIT OF SORROW** Tears of Godly sorrow brings forth repentance after it has had enough time to complete the Holy Spirit's work. The breaking and release is signaled by an outrushing of joy or laughter, The Spirit of God will use personal sorrow as a starting point and turn it into Godly sorrow. Personal sorrow is directed self-ward, but Godly sorrow other-ward. Godly intercession interacts with several anointings; sorrow, joy, warring anger, praise and worship, according to the moving of the Spirit.

.2: **THE SPIRIT OF HOLINESS: (Worship and Holy Fear)** Though there are numerous listings of the Spirit of Holiness it is hard to account it strictly as an anointing. The closer we come to experiencing God face to face the more this power is revealed. No eye has seen nor hear has heard what God has prepared for those who love Him. But now it is revealed by the Holy Spirit.- – 1Corinthians 2:9

3: **THE SPIRIT OF COMPASSION:** For the Lord is Good and His Mercies endure forever! The Goodness of God is the source of all grace and blessing. The Father's heart of forgiveness and compassion are revealed again and again throughout scripture and are at the center of all Jesus'   ministry.   Mercy,   compassion, forgiveness;   healing;   restoration;   deliverance. The mercies of God directed to weak and fallible souls is the greatest wonder of the universe!

4: **THE SPIRIT OF PRAISE AND REJOICING: (The Spirit of Joy**) The Holy Spirit turns mourning into dancing, heaviness into praise, weeping into rejoicing. There is an ultimate point in the cycle of the Holy

31

Spirit's travail when tears of sorrow turn into victory and darkness turns into the breaking dawn of hope.

5: THE SPIRIT OF ZEAL   THE SPIRIT OF JUDGMENT: SPIRIT OF BURNING   (THE ZEAL OF GOD IS AS A CONSUMING FIRE) The study of the "Zeal of God" encompasses the entire question of God's anger, wrath and judgment and those upon whom it is directed. The   anointing of righteous anger.

6: THE ANOINTING OF POWER dunamis, doo'-nam-is; from G1410; force (lit. or fig.); spec. miraculous power (usually by impl. a miracle itself):–ability, abundance, meaning, might (-ily, -y, -y deed), (worker of) miracle (-s), power, strength, violence, mighty (wonderful) work.

7: THE SPIRIT OF WISDOM AND UNDERSTANDING:

(The Spirit of Truth)   To truly discern it is to know the mind and heart of God. To know the full reality. To have this heart within you, is a guiding light of wisdom and knowledge that at once, knows the truth. In this anointing we know that God is our Father; that the Bible is his divine voice speaking the word of truth; often that human voices written or spoken, are speaking from personal vanity or from divine revelation.One next also can personally manifest these 7 spirits of God as a Holy Spirit gifting   following their personal Baptism in the Holy Spirit.

The Baptism of the Holy Spirit is generally a separate secondary experience,   after one becomes saved.

We can clearly see also all of these attributes in real Holy Spirit filled, anointed Christians now as well in the New Testament and following.Jesus had said that without Him and his Holy Spirit you can do nothing.. nothing everlasting, or significant too. yet people falsely do try to Divorce the Holy Spirit or try to substitute the Holy Spirit with false doctrines, vanities still to daySeeActs 10:38

How God anointed Jesus of Nazareth with the Holy Ghost and with power: who went about doing good, and healing all that were oppressed of the devil; for God was with him.We all do need the power, the anointing of the Holy Spirit in our life. The Greek word for anointing is chrisma, from which we have the word chrism. Chrisma appears several times in 1 John 2:20 and 27. It comes from the root word, chriô, which means to rub something or someone lightly with a substance like oil or lotion. The word christos means a person so anointed and the word chrisma refers to that by which a person is anointed. John uses chrisma in these two verses, not speaking of the object being anointed but of the instrument of anointing. Additionally, we find a word christianos in Acts 11:26, which means "one belonging to the Anointed One,"

just as Herodianos would mean "one who belongs to Herod."AND THERE IS NO SUCH THING AS A PARTIAL CHRISTIAN WHO REJECTS THE ANOINTING OF THE HOLY SPIRIT and as to why the Christians were called Christians.. We need to look at what the Bible itself says here firstly too.To be a Christian is based on the Greek word anointed one, Christos, a person in whom we can see the anointing of the Holy Spirit of Jesus Christ.. Jesus Christ himself also was baptized with the Holy Spirit, The word "Christ" is a transliteration of the Greek word christos, meaning "the Anointed One.(Acts 10:38 KJV) How God anointed Jesus of Nazareth with the Holy Ghost and with power: who went about doing good, and healing all that were oppressed of the devil; for God was with him.

Now the anointed one- Greek for Messiah (anointed one) is Christos, Christ in English. Thus, "Jesus Christ" joins a name and a title, and means

Jesus the Messiah. Christ, Messiah, Anointed One. The title "Christ" or "Anointed One" Gk. Christos "Cristov" occurs about 350 times in the New Testament..The word christos means a person HOLY SPIRIT anointed .

The Greek name for an individual "Christos" rendered "Christ" in Scripture, the basic of the term Christian now as well, comes from the Greek word "chrio" means to anoint with oil, the symbol of the Holy Spirit,Luke 4:18-19 (Wey) [Jesus:]

"The Spirit of the Lord is upon me, because He has anointed me to proclaim Good News to the poor; He has sent me to announce release to the prisoners of war and recovery of sight to the blind: to send away free those whom tyranny has crushed, to proclaim the year of acceptance with the Lord."But you have an anointing from the Holy One, and all of you know the truth. . .

.As for you, the anointing you received from him remains in you, and you do not need anyone to teach you. But as his anointing teaches you about all things and as that anointing is real, not counterfeit–just as it has taught you, remain in him. 1 John 2:20, 27;I can understand why the false Christians do not want to be associated with the name of Jesus Christ.. and the Baptism of the Holy Spirit especially when they do not know the Holy Spirit personally.Note this reality 50 percent of all the loudly professing Christians

I knew the last 50 years   made next a free will choice to permanently abandon Jesus for the world, the flesh, and also 70 percent of the people going to church they still are not real Christians too.All persons who try to serve God   solely in the flesh and are not   Holy Spirit filled, lead will next go into both gross errors and also into guilt and depression. As Jesus

Christ is our only salvation and our righteousness..Do you even know the true benefits of speaking in tongues, as to why this gift is so valuable..

"HERE ARE 10 REASONS TO PROVE WHY WE NEED THIS WONDERFUL GIFT.

1. The manifestation that came with the gift of the Holy Spirit was speaking in tongues. It wasn't the wind, fire, noise or feeling of God's presence that was evidence of the gift being received but a spirit language--believers began speaking languages of the Spirit they didn't understand. It was God's plan for the gift to function as a spirit language for His children (Acts 2:4, 11; 1 Cor. 14:2).

2. Jesus commanded us to receive the gift of the Holy Spirit. When Jesus commissioned the disciples to wait in Jerusalem until they received the promise of the Father, He didn't say, "Do this if you feel led to do so, or if it fits in your doctrinal or denominational beliefs, or if you have the time, or if you are so inclined, or if you feel comfortable about it." No! Jesus commanded them to wait until they received the gift of the Holy Spirit. Since Jesus put such importance on their receiving this gift, that's more than enough reason for every Christian to seek God until they receive it too (Acts 1:4; 5:32; John 14:16-17; Eph. 5:18).

3. The Scriptures exhort us to be filled with the Spirit and to pray in the new tongues of our spirit language. Our spirit language enables us to live in the Spirit, walk in the Spirit, be led of the Spirit, have the fruit of the Spirit, manifest the gifts of the Spirit and go from glory to glory until we are transformed into His same image (Gal. 5:22-25; Rom. 8:14; 1 Cor. 12:7-11; 14:15; Eph. 5:18; Acts 19:2; 2 Cor. 3:18).

4. A spirit language is the greatest gift the Holy Spirit can give a believer. Jesus is the greatest gift God could give for the redemption

of the world, and the Holy Spirit is the greatest gift Jesus could give to His church. Of all the resources in heaven and the eternal universe, nothing is more valuable, beneficial or important for the Holy Spirit to give the individual child of God than her own spirit language (1 Cor. 12:31; 14:4).

5. Our spirit language enables us to have spirit-to-Spirit communication with God. Humans are spirit beings clothed with flesh-and-bone bodies. While man's sin deadened the spirit, Jesus brings the spirit back to life by imparting His everlasting life into us. The Holy Spirit gives us a spirit language so we can communicate directly with God (John 4:24; 1 Cor. 15:45; Gen. 2:7; Rom. 5:12; John 3:3-5, 16).

6. Praying in tongues builds and increases our faith. Faith is the medium of exchange for all heavenly things, just as money is the medium of exchange for all earthly things. A major way to increase our faith is to pray in the tongues of our spirit language (Rom. 12:6; Jude 1:20; Mark 9:23; Matt. 9:29).

7. Praying in tongues activates the fruit of the Spirit. It's vital and beneficial to have each of the spiritual attributes become active and mature in us. Praying in tongues helps us fulfill God's predestined purpose for us to be conformed to the image of His Son (Gal. 5:22-23; 2 Cor. 3:18; 1 Cor. 13:1-13; Rom. 8:29).

8. Praying in our spirit language is the main way we fulfill the scriptural admonition to "pray without ceasing." Christians can pray in tongues at any time. If we are in a place where it isn't convenient or wise to speak out loud in tongues, we can pray with our inner man without making an audible sound (Eph. 6:18; 1 Thess. 5:17; Matt. 26:41; Luke 18:1; 21:36; 1 Cor. 14:15).

9. The Holy Spirit directs our spirit language to pray in accordance

with the will of God. Probably the only time we can be assured that we are praying 100 percent in the will of God is when we are praying in our spirit language. God always answers requests that are made in alignment with His will (Rom. 8:27; 1 John 5:14-15).

10. Praying in tongues quiets the mind. When Dr. Andrew Newberg, a neuroscientist, compared brain scans of Christians praying in tongues with Buddhist monks chanting and Catholic nuns praying, the study showed the frontal lobes--the brain's control center--went quiet in the brains of Christians talking in tongues, proving that speaking in tongues isn't a function of the natural brain but an operation of the spirit (1 Cor. 14:2, 14). "

SEVENTY REASONS
FOR SPEAKING IN TONGUES

It is amazing that many people falsely concentrate on what they or others believe, what mere men and women say on the Subject and not rather what the New testament Bible actually says .. as the devil does not want them to see and admit the Bible truth.. there are so many different and even false interpretations too on what tongues thus is -"that the gift of tongues constituted a type of " language," a series of initially unintelligible sounds that are unrelated to one's own human speech and so they need to be also interpreted. One should pray to have this interpretation too". These Bible liars and distorters would falsely have you believe that the gift of a "tongue" was simply the divinely imposed ability to communicate the gospel of Christ in a human language that the speaker had not been taught by the ordinary education process.

They are really big liars who talk about something they have no idea of what it really is still. God has given to the real Christians, those Baptized with the Holy Spirit, the gift to speak in a language that we do not know by human means. This is a gift of the Holy Spirit (1 Cor 12:10) and therefore of great help to us in praying for our own needs and the needs of others too.

Paul said: "Thank God, I speak in tongues more than any of you" (1 Cor 14:18). Through the gift of tongues, the Lord builds us up (1 Cor 14:4), enables us to utter "mysteries in the Spirit" (1 Cor 14:2), and empowers us to thank and praise Him (1 Cor 14:16-17).

The gift of tongues in the Church is a sign, also especially for unbelievers (1 Cor 14:22). Still there are different "kinds of tongues" (see 1 Cor 12:10 in the Greek).

Apostle Paul taught: "If there is no one to interpret, there should be silence in the assembly, each one praying, speaking only to himself and to God

" (1 Cor 14:28). Tongues are either interpreted for the upbuilding of the Church or are spoken in prayers only to ourselves and to God. This second kind of tongues is often called a "prayer language." One should pray for it's interpretation also.

Yes speaking in tongues proceeds from the abundance of the gift of the Holy Spirit. Tongues were the outward and audible expression of this abundance.

Moreover, these tongues, whether spoken in Jerusalem or Caesarea, were in praise of God and primarily directed to God

. As Paul was later to say, "One who speaks in a tongue does not speak to men, but to God" (1 Corinthians 14:2)." There is a river of the Holy Spirit that comes from God whose streams makes glad "believers" and fills them with joy and peace

. As a result this river gives them joy and gladness, thanksgiving and the voice of melody. Yes, Joy and gladness are the trade marks of being filled with the power of the Holy Spirit.

Christianity is not only to be understood with our hearts and minds and appreciated for its many miracles, signs and wonders but it's to be experienced through the moving of the Holy Spirit.

"John 16:7 "Nevertheless I tell you the truth; It is expedient for you that I go away: for if I go not away, the Comforter will not come unto you; but if I depart, I will send him unto you.""I believe that one of the biggest reasons that the body of Christ hasn't made a greater impact on our generation today is because of our failure to operate in the gifts of the Holy Spirit.

Without a doubt, Jesus and the first apostles used the gifts like a bell, calling men to their message and confirming that God was truly the One speaking through them". Hebrews 2:3-4 says, "How shall we escape, if we neglect so great salvation; which at first began to be spoken by the Lord, and was confirmed unto us by them that heard him; God also bearing them witness, both with signs and wonders, and with divers miracles, and gifts of the Holy Ghost, according to his own will?"

The Lord bore witness to the accuracy of their message through miracles and gifts of the Holy Spirit.In Mark 16:17-18, Jesus said all true believers would flow in the miraculous: "And these signs will follow them that believe; In my name shall they cast out devils; they shall speak with new tongues; They shall take up serpents; and if they drink any deadly thing, it shall not hurt them; they shall lay hands on the sick, and they shall recover

."The vast majority of preaching and Christian living done in the name of the Lord today is still really without the power of the Holy Spirit manifest through the gifts of the Holy Spirit. This was, is not the way the Lord Jesus Christ had intended it to be for sure.. No one can have an effective life or ministry without the power of God's Holy Spirit working in him or her. This fact can't be argued by anyone who truly believes the Bible is God's Word.

The Scriptures are replete with proof that it is "not by might, nor by power, but by my Spirit, saith the LORD of hosts" (Zech. 4:6). It is true that the Holy Spirit is still willing to move as in biblical times then there is no excuse for living lives so far removed from that great victory portrayed in God's Word.Many even religious persons, people are falsely trying to reach Heaven, serve God in their own efforts neglect God's provisions for them, God's spiritual gifts.

if you oppose tongues you are not even a Christian led by the holy Spirit. and that is your main problem still.. not being filled with the Holy Spirit.. You do Acts 2:4: "All of them were filled with the Holy Spirit and began to speak in other tongues as the Spirit enabled them.Beware of the fundamentals who are experts on speaking in toungues but have never sprayed in toungues, who clearly hate the Holy Spirit cause they are still self centered

Beware always of men and women, bullies, tormentors, control freaks, persons, civil and public servants, politicians, pastors, leaders, elders, who falsely do, will try to enslave you, oppress you, exploit you while claiming to be helping you .Covet to prophesy, and forbid not to speak with tongues. (Rom 1:16 KJV)

For I am not ashamed of the gospel of Christ: for it is the power of God unto salvation to every one that believeth; to the Jew first, and also to the Greek.(Psa 127:1 KJV) Except the LORD build the house, they labour in vain that build it: except the LORD keep the city, the watchman waketh but in vain. 2 It is vain for you to rise up early, to sit up late, to eat the bread of sorrows: for so he giveth his beloved sleep.(Prov 3:5 KJV)

Trust in the LORD with all thine heart; and lean not unto thine own understanding..(Gal 5:25 KJV) If we live in the Spirit, let us also walk in the Spirit.The Lord wants to infuse you with an anointing, by the Holy Spirit, which will propel you through every line of Satan's defense.

This is how you can overcome every situation as you receive "power from on high!" Our Lord Jesus Christ Himself was full of this power as He withstood the onslaught of the devil while fasting in the wilderness.

The Bible records that John the Baptist baptized Jesus, the Lord of Glory, in the river Jordan prior to Him praying and fasting 40 days and 40 nights. At the end of this fast Satan came to Him and tempted Him in His spirit, soul and body to sin against God. But Jesus resisted Satan's offense with the statement, "It is written!" After this, Luke 4: 14 states,

And Jesus returned in the power of the Spirit into Galilee: and there went out a fame of him through all the region round about. If Jesus, walking as a man, needed the power of the Holy Spirit to stand against the assault of the devil, I ask you, "How much more do we need the power of the Holy Spirit?" There's a Holy Spirit revival coming, and it's can also be coming even through your words, through your hands and through your life! Would you like to have God's Holy Ghost Power in your life?

If so please pray this prayer humbly. "Dear Heavenly Father. As per your promises in your word, the Bible do next baptize me with your Holy sprit, power. I accept the promise of Acts 2: 38 & 39 and the anointing power of the Holy Ghost. I ask to have the power that Apostles had received even in my life. I also do want the power to overcome Satan everyday, in all areas of life!

Jesus you are my lord so by your Holy Spirit, please fill me now and take full control of my life, my body and even my tongue. Let my tongue now also give praises to God the Father and His Holy Son, Jesus in a Heavenly language. I put myself, my all under your full control.

Amen!"(Acts 1:8 KJV) But ye shall receive power, after that the Holy Ghost is come upon you: and ye shall be witnesses unto me both in Jerusalem, and in all Judaea, and in Samaria, and unto the uttermost part of the earth. Again True Christians even these days Are Holy Ghost Baptized and they know they have received such a personal experience.. even as evidenced by speaking in tongues

Beyond the show of a doubt the devil himself firstly really hates any references to the Holy Spirit, the anointed ones, the idea that Christians do have now empowering to overcome the devil too... and so now the devil uses any of his followers, those in the fundamental religious circles too now, to now lie, twist, distort the truths. It's the frequent and methodical strategy of those people not Holy sprit filled, those people walking in the flesh that they do bash, recite against anyone who has evidenced the Holy Spirit anointing still too, we all can see these false professors own false, unscriptural doctrine and practice. It's now a charge of their "blasphemy of the Holy Spirit" and their disobedience of "touch not the Lord's anointed."The anointing is sacred, the anointing is the Holy Spirit, and all believers in Christ have the anointing of the Holy Spirit.

We must be careful what we say about our brothers and sisters in Christ.(Matthew 12:31 NKJV) "Therefore I say to you, every sin and blasphemy will be forgiven men, but the blasphemy against the Spirit will not be forgiven men.In 1 Corinthians 12 Paul lists out The Holy Spirit gifts. Any Spirit-filled Christian can eventually manifest or release any of these gifts as the Holy Spirit directs him.

Word of Wisdom – God's supernatural perspective on how to achieve His will. God's knowledge rightly applied to specific situations. Word of Knowledge – "Facts" given by God that are unknowable without revelation.The Gift of Faith – The supernatural ability to believe God without doubt. Essential to the Gift of Healing and Miracles.

The Gift of Healing – Supernatural healing through special anointing of the Holy Spirit. The Working of Miracles – A supernatural display of power that goes beyond the natural to counteract earthly and evil forces.

Discerning of Spirits – Spiritual insight into differences between the Holy Spirit, the the spirit of Man, and evil spirits at work in the earth. It is not the discerning of character faults. The Gift of Prophecy –

The forth-telling of God's utterance. It is not of the intellect but of the Spirit. It is divinely inspired and anointed words spoken by a believer.

Kinds of Tongues – This is not to be confused with the use of tongues in private prayer or worship. This refers to the ministry of tongues to others. An utterance from a believer to another in a language unknown to the speaker. (Isaiah 28:11; Mark 16:17; Acts 2:4; 10:44-48; 19:1-7; 1 Corinthians 12:10; 13:1-3; 14:2,4-22,26-31; 28:31)

Interpretation of Tongues – Supernatural power to reveal the meaning of tongues. Not a translation, but an interpretation. Tongues and Interpretation working together can be the equivalent of prophecy.

The working of these nine Gifts is for the profit and advantage of the Church. They are for the benefit of the Church and are specifically available to every believer as the Holy Spirit wills. (1Corinthians 12:7-11; 14:12). They should all be actively welcomed and expected in your life

. (1Corinthians 14:1)HOW MANY Spiritual, GIFTS from God, Jesus Christ and the Holy Spirit DO WE GET? With the exception of speaking in troupes, which is a Baptism of the Holy Spirit evidence sign, it depend on how we will next use them too?The Holy Spirit distributes His gifts to each believer severally as He wills. (1 Corinthians 12:11)

It is not up to us how many gifts we want or are willing to use but up to the Holy Spirit to give whatever He wants to whoever He wants whenever He wants. It is up to us to appreciate all of them and to allow the Holy Spirit to use us in any of them to minister to others.

The Baptism of the Holy Spirit is God's way of empowering us to manifest His love to His Church and to cleanse us and make us holy. We need therefore to acknowledge that love is necessary for the proper use of the

Gifts – faith works by love.(Galations 5:6) Love edifies others (1Corinthians 8:1) as God has shown His love for you by giving you faith to believe in and trust in and cling to and rely on Jesus. Repent of anything that would hold you back from experiencing and walking in His fullness through the Baptism in the Holy Spirit. Ask Him for it. Receive it. Freely it has been given to you – now freely give. (Matthew 10:8).

And we are witnesses of these things; and so is the Holy Spirit, whom God has given to those who obey Him. Acts 5:32 "Now we have received, not the spirit of the world, but the spirit which is of God; that we might know the things that are freely given to us of God. Which things also we speak, not in the words which man's wisdom teacheth, but which the Holy Ghost teacheth; comparing spiritual things with spiritual" (I Corinthians 2:12-13).

"Howbeit when he, the Spirit of truth, is come, he will guide you into all truth: for he shall not speak of himself; but whatsoever he shall hear, that shall he speak: and he will shew you things to come. He shall glorify me: for he shall receive of mine, and shall shew it unto you. He shall glorify me: for he shall receive of mine, and shall shew it unto you. All things that the Father hath are mine: therefore said I, that he shall take of mine, and

shall shew it unto you" (John 16:13-15). It is absolutely amazing how the Holy Spirit shows the extent of our inheritance in Christ to those who will receive the anointing. Another purpose is that the Holy Spirit may become our spiritual teacher and to bring to our memory also what He has taught us. "But the Comforter, which is the Holy Ghost, whom the Father will send in my name, he shall teach you all things, and bring all things to your remembrance, whatsoever I have said unto you" (John 14:26).

One primary purpose of the anointing of the Holy Spirit is that one may be a witness unto Christ. One is not just to be a his witness, witness about Jesus, or witness for him, but to witness UNTO him. "But ye shall receive power, after that the Holy Ghost is come upon you: and ye shall be witnesses unto me both in Jerusalem, and in all Judaea, and in Samaria, and unto the uttermost part of the earth" (Acts 1:8).

This means that when others see the person who is anointed with the Holy Spirit, they should be seeing Jesus. The anointing will also bring conviction to the "world" through the Believer. "Nevertheless I tell you the truth; It is expedient for you that I go away: for if I go not away, the Comforter will not come unto you; but if I depart, I will send him unto you.

And when he is come, he will reprove the world of sin, and of righteousness, and of judgment: Of sin, because they believe not on me; Of righteousness, because I go to my Father, and ye see me no more; Of judgment, because the prince of this world is judged" (John 16:7-11).

The word "reprove" is demonstrated when the prosecuting attorney brings proof into the court that the crime has been committed by the defendant. To be led directly by the Holy Spirit even these days is a normal Christian walk. Gal 2:2 KJV And I went up by revelation, and communicated unto them that gospel which I preach among the Gentiles.

But you have an anointing from the Holy One, and all of you know the truth. . . . As for you, the anointing you received from him remains in you, and you do not need anyone to teach you. But as his anointing teaches you about all things and as that anointing is real, not counterfeit–just as it has taught you, remain in him.

1 John 2:20, (Gal 3:1 KJV) O foolish Galatians, who hath bewitched you, that ye should not obey the truth, before whose eyes Jesus Christ hath been evidently set forth, crucified among you?2   This only would I learn of you, Received ye the Spirit by the works of the law, or by the hearing of faith

faith

Disciples of Jesus Christ were first called "Christians" in Antioch (Acts 11:26) because evidentially their behavior, activity, and speech were anointed, Christ like. (Acts 10:38 KJV) How God anointed Jesus of Nazareth with the Holy Ghost and with power: who went about doing good, and healing all that were oppressed of the devil;

for God was with him.Unfortunately over time, in the often dead, corrupted churches, the real definition of word "Christian" has lost a great deal of its real, original significance and is more often used of someone who is a religious Christian and supposedly has high moral values instead of being a true born again, Holy Spirit anointed disciple of Jesus Christ.

The Anointing Upon and Within We see clearly in Scripture that the Spirit of the Lord rested upon Jesus during His earthly ministry. Isaiah the prophet speaks of the seven manifestations of the Holy Spirit that would rest upon the Lord.

"The Spirit of the LORD shall rest upon Him, the Spirit of wisdom and understanding, The Spirit of counsel and might, The Spirit of knowledge and of the fear of the LORD (Isaiah 11:2)." There are not seven Holy Spirit's. There is only one Holy Spirit, yet

He is displayed through these seven manifestations which rested upon Jesus. The Spirit of God can also rest upon the believer in order to anoint that person to function in their assigned calling. The anointing upon a person can be increased through obedience to God and time spent in the Word and prayer.In Luke the fourth chapter

we read of the time when Jesus went and preached in the synagogue of His hometown of Nazareth. Jesus was handed the scroll of Isaiah and he deliberately found and read the text of Scripture which we identify as Isaiah 61:1, and the first part of verse 2. Jesus read to the people, saying, "The Spirit of the LORD is upon me."

This famous portion of Scripture was prophetically speaking of the coming Messiah. After reading those verses He closed the book, and gave it back to the attendant and sat down. The story in Luke tells us that all the eyes of the people in the synagogue were fixed on Him.

When reading this story we can't help but be curious as to why the people's eyes were fixed on Him. When you study Jewish customs and traditions, you find an interesting practice that took place in Jesus' day, and can still be observed in some synagogues today.

The Jews reserve a special seat in their synagogues which is kept for the appearance of the Messiah. That special chair always remains empty and no one ever sits in it. Well, after Jesus finished speaking He sat down! He actually sat in that reserved chair and it caught all the attention of those in attendance. Jesus spoke to those in the synagogue and said, "Today this Scripture is fulfilled in your hearing." He basically told them, "That Scripture is talking about Me." Jesus knew He was the Anointed One.The anointing that is upon you is for service.

God anoints you with His Spirit to empower you to do the work He has called you to do. For example, the Lord has placed an anointing upon my life for miracles of healing. This gift, which is a special anointing He gave to me, has taken me around the world in the work of the ministry

. When that anointing comes upon me and others release their faith to receive that anointing the results are always the same miracles! I've seen it happen in America and all over the world with creative miracles occurring and all types of diseases healed. Just as there is an anointing upon, there is also an anointing within. "But you have an anointing from the Holy One, and you know all things (1 John 2:20)."

"But the anointing which you have received from Him abides in you, and you do not need that anyone teach you; but as the same anointing teaches you concerning all things, and is true, and is not a lie, and just as it has taught you, you will abide in Him (1 John 2:27)."Notice we are told where the anointing abides. "But the anointing which you have received from Him abides in you."

The anointing is within us. This anointing teaches us concerning all things. Some have taken this scripture out of context and misuse it to imply that we do not need instructors or teachers. However, Jesus is the head of the church and He established the five ministry offices as gifts to the church

. The ministry office of the teacher is one of the five offices mentioned in Ephesians the fourth chapter. So, we need teachers. To reject the biblical ministry of the teacher is to reject a precious gift from God.The anointing within you is for guidance and protection. It teaches you what is from God and what is not.

"These things I have written to you concerning those who try to deceive you (1 John 2:26)." The anointing within you protects you from deception, just as a virus software program protects your computer from malicious infections. When corrupt teaching is presented the anointing within you goes off on the inside of you like an alarm. The anointing says, "Watch out, something is not right there!" When something is wrong you have an uneasy feeling on the inside. When something is right you should have a peaceful, velvety smooth feeling on the inside

.The anointing within helps you to know all things. The more sensitive a person becomes to the anointing within, the more success they will have in making the right decisions in life. We should use our brain and utilize the best of our mental abilities. However, the anointing resides within your spirit, not within your physical brain.

Yes, the anointing of God certainly affects the brain which influences us to think godly thoughts. But some decisions we have to make in life go beyond the ability of one's brain to solve. Who to marry? Where to work? Where to go to church? What color should I paint the house?

The answer to these types of questions should be measured through the anointing that resides within us.Other questions such as, "Was that prophecy that person gave me from God, or not?" or, "How do I know if God has called me to the ministry?" The Holy Spirit will guide us through the anointing that God has placed within us.

There's no need to be in the dark when it comes to knowing God's will and purpose. Let the anointing within you help settle the perplexing questions and choices you face. You can always trust the anointing of the Holy Spirit that abides within you to point you in the right direction.The better developed you become to recognizing the inward anointing, the greater will be your ability to carry the glory of God

. **Understand that the anointing within you is what supports the potential anointing that can rest upon you.** For example, some ministers have had a strong anointing upon them. This anointing initially came through God's grace in which He bestowed spiritual gifts through His own choice. The gifts and callings of God are irrevocable (Romans 11:29).

These spiritual gifts were received by men and women through an act of God's grace. But some individuals have had failures, with some falling from ministry and never fully recovering. How does a tragedy like this happen? The reason a spiritual collapse takes place is because the inward anointing comprised of biblical morals, holy character, humility, and other spiritual attributes was deficient in that person's life.

The inward anointing was not valued or developed, so such an individual could not support the weight of the anointing of God that is able to come upon a person. We see this clearly in the life of Samson. What a mighty anointing that he had that would come upon him! The nation of Israel had never seen anything like it before. But we all know the unfortunate outcome of his life. Its how we finish that's important, not necessarily how we start out

. **It is up to us to train ourselves to be diligent and instantly obedient to following the inward anointing.** By doing so we will partake of the fruits of obedience which God richly brings forth. May the Lord bless you as you walk in His anointing whi

1. SALVATION

At the point of initial salvation, all believers are filled with the Holy Spirit when we invite Jesus to come into our heart. God anoints all believers to hear from God for themselves, to discern between truth and error and to successfully live the Christian life.

The next step after initial salvation is the Baptism of the Holy Spirit, which is to be "endued with power" from on High (Luke 24:49). Salvation = filled with the SpiritBaptism of the Holy Spirit = endued with the Spirit.Both salvation and the Baptism in the Holy Spirit involve being filled with God's Spirit, although the Baptism is a deeper infilling or level of the Spirit.

A believer who does not believe in the baptism of the Holy Spirit and speaking in tongues is still saved, loves God and has His presence living on the inside of them. But they could have so much more of God by receiving the Baptism of the Holy Spirit. The Baptism is an enduement of power and is the door or entrance to operating in the Gifts of the Spirit.

The Baptism of the Spirit enables the believer to walk in greater victory in their Christian life, to live a life where healings, miracles and the supernatural is a common part of life, and to enter into deeper levels in God in worship, the Word and communion with the Holy Spirit.

2. MINISTRY

The second level of anointing is when God anoints the believer for the particular ministry that God has called him or her to do. Everyone in the Body of Christ is called to be in ministry.

There is to be no competition or jealousies, or comparisons among believers, as each of us is given an assignment from the Master (Jesus) to fulfill. Not all are called to clergy ministry, but all are called to fulfill a specific ministry assignment that God has given each of us to do.

The believer does not have to go in their own strength to minister, but goes in the Name of the Lord and is endued with the power and anointing of the Holy Spirit to carry out their particular ministry assignment. God's anointing for ministry equips them with the skill, ability, wisdom and favor to function in their area of ministry.

God's anointing for ministry will bring about fruitfulness. Often times a person called to a ministry involving speaking before an audience literally feels an anointing descend upon them as they begin to minister, and they may even be a changed person full of boldness and authority while under the influence of that anointing if normally they are shy and quiet.

Then after 2 or 3 hours after ministering, the anointing may lift. The same example could hold true of those anointed to prophesy. Normally they may be reserved and quiet, but when the anointing comes on them for ministry, they are a completely different person until the anointing lifts after they are finished ministering. People called to the healing ministry, while under the influence of the anointing for ministry, may feel literal heat, electricity and power coming out of their hands, or may operate in words of knowledge, and be unusually bold.

3. AUTHORITY

Being anointed with authority in the Spirit is the 3rd level that is higher and deeper than ministry alone. When flowing in this anointing, your words have the power to plant or uproot.

Your words carry weight, and none of your words fall to the ground. Your words have the power to decree and command (as led by the Spirit and coming into agreement with and repeating what the Spirit is saying, and speaking under the influence of the Holy Spirit. (It's not from the flesh commanding or decreeing things.

If it's just the flesh, it will produce no fruit.) When you decree and command, then God backs up what you say. The anointing for authority also involves the area of declaring deliverance to the captives, and the captives are delivered and chains are broken.

The anointing for authority involves creative miracles – decreeing and speaking things that are not as though they were, commanding them to be, and it happens just as you say. The anointing for authority involves an anointing for breakthrough. Authority is the kingly anointing – to rule and reign with Christ and know who you are in Christ.

To make decrees in the heavenly realms, and it comes to pass. To have authority over demons and satan, and all powers of wickedness. To cast out devils. To raise the dead. Authority also involves taking charge of distractions and people who would mock or cause interruptions in services, which weaken the flow of the Spirit and thus grieves the Holy Spirit.

You must take charge of distractions from people who try to prevent others from hearing the Word, from distractions that hinder people from hearing the Gospel of Salvation and receiving Christ as Savior, from distractions that make it difficult for people to receive their healing and miracle, and distractions that discourage others in regards to receiving the Baptism of the Holy Spirit or distract the flow of the operation of the Gifts of the Spirit.

Taking authority in this type of situation would involve stopping ministering for a minute and openly telling the troublemakers [those are my words not what Benny said] to either be quiet or leave, and if need be, having the ushers escort them out.

It also involves making it clear that there are to be no cell phones ringing and people talking, no constant talking to your neighbor, whispering, goofing off, constantly going in and out of the sanctuary during the worship and the preaching of the Word unless it's a dire medical emergency.

The anointing for authority involves situations in which Satanic plants are sent to churches and meetings to try to cause distractions and the demise of the pastors and leadership.Sometimes people who cause distractions are not a Satanic plant, it's just that they can be rude, inconsiderate, immature, disrespectful and have not been taught to keep quiet and not talk to their neighbor, or on the cell phone, during the worship and preaching.

I'm talking about people who are in the habit of talking during most of the service, and they do this all the time. When I was a child we were taught to not talk or goof off during the worship and the Word.

If we got restless we could color in a coloring book or read a book. It seems like today so many parents don't teach their children to be quiet during the services, and they let them talk and run around.Sometimes distractions are caused by demons manifesting in people.

There's a time to cast out demons (as Jesus demonstrated in His ministry). Then there is a time when you are to command the demons to be silent (as Jesus also did in His ministry).On rare occasions, the anointing for authority involves, when directed by the Spirit, pronouncing judgment on those who rise up to try to destroy the work of God, and the Lord backs up your words and He carries out the judgment. An example is Ananias and Sapphira.

The apostle Peter and other apostles pronounced a judgment on them for not only lying to them, but for also lying to the Holy Ghost. Another example is when Elijah pronounced a judgment on the young boys who mocked him because of his baldness. He probably was literally bald, but the Scriptures imply that the mocking was deeper than just making fun of his lack of hair, but mocking the anointing on his life.

In the ministry of William Branham, there was a situation that arose in one of the meetings in which he pronounced a judgment (by the leading of the Spirit) upon a certain man. This man had come up to the stage in the healing line, claiming that he had cancer and for William Branham to lay hands on him so that he would be healed. The man lied – he did not have cancer.

His intent was to make a false claim about having cancer, in order to "expose" Branham as being a false prophet (because he didn't believe that God reveals things to His prophets by the words of knowledge). The man was out to prove that Branham just "made up" all those words of knowledge about people.

When the man claimed to be sick with cancer, the Holy Spirit told Branham that the man was a fake and was lying, and then Branham told the man in front of everyone there that he lied about having cancer.

Then Branham pronounced a judgment on the man for lying not only to him, but to the Holy Ghost, and told him that since he lied about having cancer, that cancer would come on his body immediately and he would be dead by the next day. It happened exactly as what Branham pronounced.

A curse and a judgment are two different things.A curse is a prayer or verbal words intending injury, harm or misfortune to come to someone (usually based on hate, jealousy, and wicked intents of the heart).

We are not called to curse. A judgment is the discernment between good and evil, what is right and what is wrong, and based on the evidence and situation, making a judicial decision and pronouncing a verdict and the consequence/punishment (if applicable) according to the laws established by God. The authority to pronounce a judgment is granted to you from a Higher Authority (God).

It applies to true God ordained Apostles who walk in greater levels of authority. The anointing to pronounce a judgment is not the same thing as Matthew 7:1 "Judge not, lest ye be judged." In Matthew 7:1, it's not referring to a judicial decision based on right and wrong, but to be critical and despise someone and their shortcomings, and to be very condemning of others, while you yourself are not perfect.

This type of judging involves pride – of pointing out the faults of others, while ignoring the plank in your own eye. This type of judgment involves judging others for their actions when you don't know all the facts and have not heard all sides of the story, nor have been in their shoes. This differs from a judgment made by a judge and jury in a courtroom, based on discerning and separating the facts and reaching a verdict. On very rare occasions is a judgment pronounced.

The church, as a whole, is not ready for things to go back to the way it was in the early Church in Acts. The glory of the Lord has the power to heal and bring about miracles. Yet one can also perish in the Glory by things such as irreverence, profaning the holy things of God, lying to the Holy Ghost, and trying to destroy someone's ministry or discredit them.

Whenever the Lord is to anoint you for service in the administration of HIS kingdom, it is not exclusive to gifting {charismata} alone, but is smeared upon our character and manhood before ministry as well. Surely, it is a delicate process that encompasses much more than the visibility of being in the work of the ministry {For some, it is public success versus private failure}, but with the compositional and {spiritual} chemical changes within us for maximum yield in the steadfast counsel {Proverbs 8:14} of God.

As in the scriptural confirmation of Acts 1:8, the saints receive power after the Holy Ghost is come upon them, but with a progressive unfolding indeed. Here, there are those that are specifically anointed & appointed in ministry forJerusalem, Judea, and for others, Samaria, and the uttermost parts of the world.

There is a difference or distinction of clarity in anointing for one that has a more localized grace to remain in Jerusalem, and there is a difference and distinction of clarity in anointing in those given to the nations.

Though the measure of rule is distinct, and the anointing more or less intense upon the assignment given, it is never to conclude that one individual is more or less important than the other because of the level of anointing and responsibilities that God has measured out to you

.It is never to be assumed that you are less fortunate for not having a million souls won to the Lord in your lifetime, or more important for having the largest assembly in the city.

Everyone is not given to high finance, or multi-million dollar projects, or to be executive directors of Fortune 500 firms. Neither is all appointed to servile workloads, manual dexterity, or profound business acumen.Truth is, the level or dimension of the anointing is tied into several key kingdom factors, including

the MULTIPLICATION of Grace in your life, the MAGNIFICATION of the glory of the Lord in your life, the plan and purpose of God for your life, the tailor - made expression the Lord would have you to BE and to DO, your measure of Rule based on 2 Corinthians 10:12-18

, HIS-divine assignment for your LIFE, and the way in which the Lord is specifically dealing with you therein. These and other important aspects of HIS abundant LIFE becomes a compound anointing within you, and not forgetting, {RESPONSIBILITY}, or

our RESPONSE to HIS Ability, our surrender to HIM, and simple obedience in all things of HIM...Bear in mind though, we do not want to approach this from a WORK's Mentality, which is rooted in a sin consciousness.

For if the anointing were predicated on our mere performance, you would have a field day with folks exclaiming through their measuring stick who is more or less anointed from the human sphere, producing competition instead of the context of proper recognition.

You would have poor, inferior, and external motivation leading to division against the saints, preference over principle, and more, all resulting in who we deem or esteem to be more anointed or less...But remember we are relating to you, the corporate body of Christ, that though there is a distinction of purpose and provision of the anointing upon His precious people, that we leave the anointing department {smile} to the HOLY SPIRIT.

For the Lord calls, Anoints, and Divinely Appoints. It is the Lord's doing, and we simply embrace this as so.There is no need, nor any deep need, to prove who is more anointed or less. Again, assignments are different, the grace upon one life is more intense or less in a given area, the glory of the Lord as the Spirit reveals upon ones life at His choosing, the manifest presence and power of God, etc.

All of these things we trust the Holy Spirit to do in His choosing, His timing, and in God's way...Let everything be done unto the glory of the Lord, decently and in order, and for HIS name...amen...As we explore briefly the Old or First Testament, we discover that there were basically three types of ministries anointed for service.

Though the Lord would never limit his precious ointment and fresh oil to a select few, the purpose here is to highlight that God does anoint for service, and in the broader more wider spectrum, the Lord pours out of his spirit unto whosoever will {Joel says ALL flesh}.

For he is gracious to whom gracious, and merciful to whom merciful. He anoints the most unlikely set of characters outside of the range of our orientation and perception. He anoints the unsanctified, those that do not fit into our group thinking. He anoints the dissatisfied, those that may find a deep need for a dietary modification other than what they are use to getting every Sunday.He discovers within them a quickening passion and a pursuit of purpose.

He sees potential or potency within us, that which appears latent and dormant inside, yet about to be erupted like a divine tsunami. He speaks into our realm from his, as eternity invades time, and brings to manifestation the proceeding word for our life {Matthew 4:4}.

For he has already created everything good and very good in 6 days, and is only manifesting what he has already created. All are saved, and all are healed, the whole world has been purchased with his blood

. HE did it! That settles that!Before there was ever a war, the battle had already been won. Before you ever experienced a problem, there was already a solution. Before there was ever a sickness, you were already healed. According to Isaiah 53:5 and 1 Peter 2:24, you are and were healed.

So, between youARE and you WERE, say with me, I AM! Whether mankind understands this or not or not, it does not stop, circumvent, nor negate the steadfast, massive, irresistible, and unending counsel of the Lord from coming to pass. He sees the done deal, and has covered the whole earth with the knowledge of HIS glory as the waters cover the sea. Isaiah 11:9; Habakkuk 2:14.

Unlike frail and mortal man, God does not discard or waste a thing. If he is anointing you, it is not without purpose. If he is anointing you, it is not without process. If he is anointing you, it is not without promotion. If he is anointing you, it is not without posterity.

Whenever he pours forth his fresh oil, it is not to be wasted, nor to be found useless. There is always a significant importance in what the Lord is doing for you, to you, in you, and through you. There is always an expected end {Jeremiah 29:11; Philippians 1:6} to what the Lord begins.All the ends of the world shall remember and return unto the Lord:

and all the kindred's of the nations shall worship before thee. For the kingdom is the Lord's: and he is the governor among the nations. Psalms 22:27-28 {Isaiah 25:6-8}He anoints the foolish five fold ministry, you know, those in 1 Corinthians 1:26-28

..."For you see your calling, brethren, how that not many wise men after the flesh, not many mighty men, not many noble, are called: But God has chosen {selected, foreordained in his predetermined counsel} the {1} foolish things of the world to confound the wise; and God has chosen the {2} weak things of the world to confound the things which are mighty: And {3} base things of the world, and things which are {4} despised, has he chosen, yea, and {5} things which are not {or nothing}, to bring to nothing things that are. 1 Corinthians 1:26-28.Did you get that beloved?

He has a whole stream of ministry in the earth that is not defined nor confined to ecclesiastical thinking. He has anointed the most foolish, weak, base, despised, and that which is regarded as nothing, that no flesh would glory in his sight!" They may not fit the bill, and may lack the criteria for being accepted into the masses, but one thing is for certain, "The Lord does not call the qualified, but qualifies the called!"In the Old or First Testament, there is the highlighting of three important {or 3-fold} ministries for anointing which is, the priest, prophet, and king.

The priests ministered to the Lord on behalf of the nation producing peace. The prophet represented the Lord before the people producing righteousness. And the king ruled in authority producing joy.

If you wish to scramble these ministries for a moment, you'd get the prophet, priest, and king. Or righteousness, peace, and joy in the Holy Ghost {Romans 14:17 - the Kingdom of God}.Here, it testifies in the New Covenant that the kingly, priestly, and the prophetic anointing is resident within the Christ, the hope {anticipation and expectation} of glory - Colossians 1:27

. Here, it is resident within the saints, the active rhythm of the Spirit, the river, and the anointing of the Lord, that not only is received but is also released.For I ask you, "Have you received the Holy Ghost since you've believed? Good, now let me ask you another question

. Have you released the Holy Ghost since you've received?As we are sharing here, some of you have not spoken or releases from your mouth through your belly the word of the Lord in ages {as it seems} and are being captivated in your mind over that which is instead of Christ {2 Corinthians 10:4-5}. That's right some of you right now need to open your mouth and prophetically proclaim the acceptable year of the Lord in your midst.

It is time, O, high time, to speak what he is saying as the Lord is the apostle and high priest of our profession {homologia - same word, speaking the same thing}. Hebrews 3:1Prepare now to prophesy, prophesy, prophesy, the counsels of God, the voice of the Lord, and the sound of his manifest presence among you

.Decree through your lips what "THUS SAITH the Lord," for your LIFE and speak what he has or is now speaking to you!Declare the word of the Lord that what he has spoken concerning you, is coming to pass! That all has been done in the 6 days of creation, and HE is only manifesting now in our appointed time what HE has already DONE {Done Deal - the Finished work of GOD - Genesis 2}.

Every promise of the Father is simply becoming a manifestation in our time from the eternity of the Lord. His time is always on time.Speak it, declare it, prophesy it, proclaim it, decree it, and release the river of the Lord from within, release the streams of life from within your belly in the name of the Lord!

He that believes on HIM as the scripture says, out of your belly shall flow as rivers of living water.Let the rivers flow, flow, flow. He has put them within you, to come forth, come forth, come forth, O river of God! Come forth and water the nations! Spring forth, O Naba and Nabiy {The prophetic dimension within you}, come forth as a fountain of life.O, river of the Living God, the Lord would declare your release this day! This day is the day of salvation and the accepted time. The TIME to Favor you has COME! You are Highly Favored {FLAVORED, roasted, marinated, pickled, sauteed, and glazed in HIS glorious presence}...

DAVID'S FIRST ANOINTING: 30   FOLD

The first of David's progression - succession began in Jesse {his father's} house: In 1 Samuel 16:1, the Lord asked Samuel the prophet how long would he mourn for king Saul {Soul}, seeing he had rejected him from reigning over Israel.

He also spoke to Samuel to fill his horn {symbol of power and strength} with oil {obviously, a greater measure to pour} and go to Jesse's house where He has provided a king among his sons. In the first anointing, bear in mind the test of preparation, even for the prophet whom is to recognize distinctly the Lord's choice.

One test of the prophet here is in the expectation of what appears to be God's choice, not based on the stature and countenance of men. If Samuel had become familiar with his presumption of a selected king, Eliab would have made a great choice.

After all, he had the look and build, but remember the test was for Samuel too, as he was just closing the door of mourning for king Saul. God did not want Samuel to speak prophetically out of familiarity over the appearance of men, as Saul was once chosen by the people

head and shoulders. In the process of the first anointing, the Lord refuses the outward appearance of men, but looks on the heart. That was Samuel's test, too. Now, let's look at David's inception into this new dimension...

Now that seven sons of Jesse had passed through the apparent inspection for the right candidate, and in obedience to the Lord for having sent

Samuel there in the first place, Samuel turns his attention to a ruddy little kid name Davi

David is the youngest of Jesse's sons whom joyfully attended the sheep. {Pastor's heart - Psalms 23 and...until you confront, contend, and conquer your Goliath, you are simply a shepherd boy}...Before the actual pouring of anointing oil, David was relinquished from his duty with the sheep by his father, which is a key principle in the first anointing. For there is anointing in instruction.

This is something a lot of local saints and believers can learn from today as the Lord appoints local elders into their life. The same with the Acts pattern of apostleship, eldership, and discipleship releasing the Spirit of HIS sonship {Sonship unto the Lord, and sonship in appointed ministries} as true authority is to be relational.

NOTICE THE THREE IMPORTANT DEVELOPMENTS OF DAVID'S NEWLY APPOINTED PROGRESSION

1 Samuel 16:11-13

1 - From the hillside - from tending the sheep - David was not a part of the original fellowship of the selected gathering, the finer choice of men, and this could be the same with you. You may not have been selected first by godly and great men in your spiritual upbringing, and perhaps have been overlooked and disregarded entirely by others. But your willing and faithful service in private prepared you for service in public. Your willingness to serve precedes the anointing for greater service.

2 - He was anointed in his adolescence or youth, way before ascending the throne: It took some years before David actually began to rule, but this principle here speaks of being anointed in what some would call

immaturity. In other words, many place a premium on age, height, size, history, credit, status, etc.

Even though David was anointed for kingship, he had to gradually mature in his expression and character, reigning, learning how to stay alive from the hands of Saul, too. As the scripture says, "Let no man despise your youth," the Lord was teaching us that the calling begin before birth itself, but the anointing comes in process of development. Before you are appointed, you are called and equipped through becoming anointed.

3 - He was anointed in the midst of his brethren, not behind the hills: David did not become anointed out of sight, but in the company of the brethren. This is important in the principle of confirmation, as when it comes to the local church, we sometimes find lone stars arising and shining apart from the group, ready to announce that the Lord had sent them this way. Sure, the Lord may call you out of sight, and confirm you openly later.

But here, the principle teaches us that confirmation not only comes through the prophecy of scripture, or the leading of His Holy Spirit, but in the company of the brethren {there, confirmation takes on a greater substance, from affirmation, to ordination into your destination}.For there are some things, which the Lord will not reveal to you in private, but only in the Corporate anointing.

With David, it was to be witnessed by others and later testified of a truth. Not forgetting, it was to prove among all, that the primary characteristic of David's first anointing was that the LORD LOOKS ON THE HEART, not on the outward as man does. Therefore, the Lord would disrobed and dismantled the thinking of carnal reasoning, making a show of it openly that his choice is not as man chooses. John 18:37

After the first anointing, David was persecuted by Saul. For one thing, one does not have to literally abdicate the throne in order to be demoted.

The scripture had already stated that Saul had slain his thousands, and David his ten thousands. The war against David continued, as a jealous pride filled king Saul had already been rejected by God. This is one reason why the Lord chose David over Saul, as David was a man of humility, and Saul, well, he was not. There is much to learn from the first to the second anointing. Let us continue in our discussion, which follows...

DAVID'S SECOND ANOINTING: 60 FOLD

David received his second anointing as confirmed in 2 Samuel 2:4. The men of Judah {praise} came to anoint David as king over the house of Judah. At that time,

David was notified that king Saul was buried. In this, we see that there is an anointing of {Judah} praise when we acknowledge that Saul {the flesh} has been put to death. For in all honesty, many brethren have not progressed in the anointing of their calling, because of the flesh, or spelled backwards without the letter "H" it is SELF.

Saul, the works of the flesh, must be put to death by the affirmation of praise {Judah}, a genuine joy of having put to death the deeds of our body

. Yes beloved, there is a powerful anointing to be released through the putting away of the flesh. There is an anointing of power, which recognize the flesh as having no authority over us. The flesh and all of its dictates have been joyfully put to death. There arises a new anointing in Hebron {the seat of association: liken to fellowship of the Spirit especially when Saul has been put to death}.

For Hebron is in Judah, or true fellowship in the Spirit is in the praises of God, and not the glory of flesh {1 Corinthians 1:29}. And, there are chiefly two kinds of praises. One, is Judah, and the other, Judas, both means praise. Judas is praise from the head, and not from the heart. Judas betrays Jesus, but Judah portrays him.

True praise in Hebron {the genuine fellowship of the Spirit}, will acknowledge Saul's death, and give glory to the Lord. A profound impact of the anointing of David during Saul's burial reveals many truths today.

Even though there was a long war between the house of Saul and the house of David, David waxed stronger and stronger, and the house of Saul waxed weaker and weaker. {2 Samuel 3:1, 10}... He must increase, we must decrease {John 3:30}...You are being anointed in the house of praise. Praise is becoming a weapon of warfare, and praise has become a way of life. Praise confounds the enemy {2 Chronicles 20}, and praise IS the LORD {Jeremiah 17:14}.

DAVID'S THIRD ANOINTING: 100 - fold:

David is anointed king over all of Israel. At Hebron {seat of association or fellowship}, David makes a league with the elders who had came from Israel. Here, I see the importance of covenant relationship as he enters into the THIRD anointing. This anointing is the THIRD DAY-CHURCH, the corporate man, the corporate Christ and many-member son.

This third anointing is vital to David, as he is acknowledged by the elders, taking us back to the principle of Jesse's house when his brothers witnessed his first anointing.Here, David takes on his greatest anointing, the third if you will.

He has risen from adolescence and childhood, though immaturity is not always impurity. He has been processed in his young life, to ascend the throne. He has later come to the second dimension of his life and ministry, from the memory of Saul and all of Saul's antagonism, to the death of Saul and the anointing of king over the house of Judah.

He is anointed in Hebron, a strategic place of association and fellowship. It is here that the purity of a new dimension arose as Saul is no longer a nagging hassle or quarrel.Though there was still a brief resistance from Saul's house, David's second anointing affirmed that Saul {flesh} was defeated from his life forever. {1 John 2 - little children, young men, and fathers - I wish I had time}

In the THIRD anointing, David reigns over all, Judah and Israel. In David or HIS third anointing, there is no divided kingdom. Israel became exalted before the Lord, and the Philistines {rolling in the dust} knew that David was anointed as king over Israel.

2 Samuel 5:17Even in David's third anointing, the Philistines continued to act out their behavior amid true defeat. Each new level of anointing will bring a level of confrontation to the call upon your life. For in David's third anointing, the warfare did not necessarily cease, and at times it got very intense

But the difference was, that David was anointed in that third realm as the overcomer, king over all. You have him as king of praise and fellowship, and king of "He shall rule as God - Israel! {Galatians 6:16}...

True UNITY of the Spirit will give no place for any stronghold to resist. As the oil from the beard of Aaron, the brethren dwell together in unity - Psalms 133:1-3}.In this third dimension, David is one with God and the brethren, vertical and horizontal, forming the shape of the cross. In the third anointing, the glory is seen in the corporate man.And thank God for your promotion into a greater corporate glory than before.

The third anointing enables us to work together as a T.E.A.M. Spirit with God, regardless, God's ATM {Apostolic Team Ministry}... David and the elders, accountability, covenant, and mutual oneness. This is also a realm of ONE-der-ful, the Oneness of God's regional purpose and plan, and not alone one spec or isolated people in the corner of the city.This is bigger than just having a local church, this is God's regional purpose and corporate vision for the whole region. This is an apostolic mobilization through the anointing of co-ruling together through covenant.

THE 3rd Anointing is here BELOVED, the church corporately is not alone to move into that third dimension, but is released of the quickening spirit to minister from this dimension of grace and glory...Some things we are not coming into, but coming from...selah

May the quickening Spirit NOW make MANIFEST {Manifest what you MANNA-Feast} from the 3rd Dimension the radiant life and glory of the King of kings in all that He IS and all that He DOES!!!Church as we know it is changing, from glory to glory, from conception to perfection, from the cross to the throne, from Moses' Tabernacle to Solomon's Temple .

We have to learn to be sensitive to the anointing. In the anointing of the Lord Jesus Christ, we mentioned how the anointing upon Him is without measure. However, He gives the anointing by measures to us. The anointing upon our lives is increased measure upon measure, as we prove faithful to the anointing.

The fullest potential of the anointing we can aspire to in whatever office we stand in is the anointing without measure – the same as the anointing upon Jesus' life. That means if God called you to be a prophet aim to reach the measureless anointing in that office, if God called you to be a teacher, aim for that.

Seek the anointing upon your life to increase until it is measureless. Now that is your aim. Jesus made a statement in Jn. 14:12, Most assuredly, I say to you, he who believes in Me, the works that I do he will do also; and greater works than these he will do, because I go to the Father. This implies that now the Holy Spirit is sent without measure. The Holy Spirit has been sent in Acts 2 as prophesied without measure. He is now pouring out on all flesh.

The potential is there for people to reach into that measureless anointing that Jesus had. Some people have moved in their respective office to a realm quite close to that. When you move into the ministry of signs and wonders, you have to be very precise to follow instructions from God.

There is another incident in William Branham's life when he was called to pray for a sick person. That person was just lying on the bed. Nothing happened when he prayed over him. He did it again and nothing happened. They were wondering what was happening.

Then he just sat around. There was a grand mother and the parent of the child there.

Then finally after some time, he wondered why nothing was happening and he was waiting. He was just sitting down. Then after a while, he came and prayed and then it worked - a miracle took place.

That person got up immediately. When asked why, he said the Lord gave him a vision. He saw the grand mother sitting on this chair and the father sitting on that chair.

Then he saw himself coming in and laying hands and pronouncing that healing, then walking off. The first time when he did it the grand mother was in a wrong position. She was in a different place and not exactly fitting the vision.

That is why nothing happened. He was waiting and waiting for them to get into the position that he saw exactly in the vision. Then only the healing took place. That was the position that you got to be in. These are what I call peculiarities.

As we move into the anointing, you have to move exactly as God showed you - no less, no more.

There have been men and women who have moved into levels of anointing close to the level of Jesus Christ in the office God has called them. Every minister called by God should aspire to reach into that anointing without measure.

However there are principles to move into that measureless anointing.

We all start with a measure of anointing God placed on our lives. God is not going to give you the measureless anointing immediately. There must be testing; there must be proving and there must be faithfulness shown. God will give a deposit of anointing upon our life up to a certain level.

Then as you are faithful to flow in it, as you are faithful to function in it, then God gives another measure. Then at that greater measure God will test your faithfulness. God will see whether you flow in it. What happens if you are not faithful? You remain at the measure you have been last given.

Let me illustrate with something you could identify with. Let say that you have been given the measure of the anointing where you would be able to prophesy in public. However, every time the anointing and the Word of God came, you resisted it.

Do not think that when the anointing comes, it is going to force you to do something. It does not force you. It just prompts you and the obedience must be yours. As the anointing comes, the person resists it the first time. Later in a different meeting, the same thing comes again.

That person resists the prompting of the Holy Spirit again. That would be quenching the Spirit of God. That person can go on out of shyness, out of fear of publicity, out of whatever reason. He could justify his disobedience but that is not acceptable to God. He could give a natural reason and God would not accept it.

The years could pass by and that person will still be the same. The measure of the anointing given to him was not allowed to function.

The gift of God in such a person's life can never be perfected. You have to grow into the perfect operation of the gift. The Corinthians had the gifts of God but they were not operating them perfectly. This shows us that the operation and perfection of the gift depend on us not on God.

Paul never question that the gifts that the Corinthians had were not from God. He acknowledged that they were from God but he wrote that he would show them a more perfect way to operate those gifts.

The operation and perfection of a gift depends on us not on God. It is our responsibility. Let us say the same person with the measure of anointing to prophesy publicly began to flow in that gift regularly whenever the anointing is there.

Sooner or later, God is going to promote him or her. He is going to give you a greater measure of anointing to move into something else. God tests and proves us to know whether we are faithful or not.

Now for those in the ministry, when you stand to minister, God may give you words of knowledge. You resist giving them since you rather just preach and teach. Perhaps it is in a home fellowship or in a smaller meeting and the word of knowledge comes to you.

You resist giving the word. You ask, "What happens if no body respond?" For the next ten years, you remain that way until you obey

. When you obey and you are faithful in that gift, a greater measure of that anointing will develop in your life. You could flow into a greater measure. It will grow from measure to measure, faith to faith, glory to glory.

We must not stop. We must grow until we arrive at the perfect function of a ministry that God has for us. God could give you a ministry of prophesying over people and every time the anointing comes, you could sense God telling you to act on the prompting.

However, all these things need a human response. You may say, "No, I do not want to do that. I do not feel like doing that." You resist and you quenched the Spirit of God

. If you keep on doing that ten years later you will still be where you are. You would not have progressed. If you are not even faithful to the measure God gives to you, there is no point in talking about the measureless anointing.

Unless you are faithful to the measure God gives you will not have more. Growth in the anointing comes with faithfully moving in the measure you already have. For example, when God first started operating the word of knowledge in my life, I have to faithfully give it.

When it comes, I will say, "All right God is showing that this is the category of the sickness He wants to heal," and I faithfully gave it.

Whether people respond or not, that is their responsibility. Whether you respond or not is your responsibility. You have to faithfully give it. I found something started happening.

The more I give the more it came. The more it came and the more I give out, it gets sharper and sharper. As I continued in it, later, I found out that it began to operate with another side effect.

At first it operates with what I call the side effect of tangibility - I sense it on my body. Later it operates together with vision. It reached a certain point where it started operating with vision.

When that operates with vision, it reaches a greater form of accuracy that can take place. That comes because of faithfulness.

The anointing can be measured. The anointing enables us to do the works of Jesus. The anointing can be increased. Just as we grow from faith to faith, from glory to glory, and from grace to grace, we also can grow in the level of anointing in our life. In addition, the Holy Spirit is received in measures.

We can measure the amount and the level of anointing that operates in our life. There are different degrees, different measures of the anointing. That measure of the anointing we are talking about here now is the measure of the anointing that God gives you to operate. Lets illustrate: God could call you to operate in the measure of ten volts of anointing.

You have a ten volts measure of the anointing. As you move in your anointing, sometimes you find that you were not up to it.

You did not spend enough time with God. Alternatively, the response from people to your ministry fluctuates. Sometimes they have more faith in you but sometimes they have less faith in the anointing that God has placed in your life. In some meetings, they have high expectancy but in some meetings low expectancy.

Although the anointing in your life is about ten volts, sometimes it flows at eight volts, sometimes at three and sometimes at ten. The level of anointing depends on the type of meeting that you are conducting, the expectancy level of the people and the level of your own preparedness.

THE WILL OF GOD

Although the will of God is for you to operate at ten volts, it does not mean you will operate at the level of ten volts everywhere you go. The anointing upon is not twenty-four hours. When the anointing upon is not functional in your life, it will be lifted off you. It will not be upon you all the time. If the anointing is upon you all the time, you cannot sleep.

Even if the measure of anointing that you have is ten volts, remember, it still has to function according to the will of God. It depends on the will of God whether God wants you to operate at that type of meeting. If there is no need for the anointing to manifest then the anointing will not manifest

. For example, if you are going for supper, obviously the need for the anointing is not there. Otherwise, if the anointing of ten volts is upon you, you could hardly order your meal. Every time you want to say something, you utter, "The Spirit of the Lord." The anointing comes only when there is a need for it. It depends on the will of God to manifest the anointing although the fullest potential you could move in is the measure of anointing God has given you. The first cause is the will of God.

PREPAREDNESS

Then the other cause is your preparedness. Sometimes you may not be more prepared than the other times. Sometimes you may be able to spend time waiting on God more than other times.

During that time, you have spent more time waiting on God. In your preparedness, you are more able to tap into the full measure of the anointing on your life. If you have done all the necessary preparation that you could for a meeting and if you are a ten volts anointed minister, you will flow at the level of ten volts subject to the other third reason.

You have these ten volts in your life. Sometimes maybe during the day you are running about and doing too many things. Perhaps you have an evangelistic meeting in Japan. You flew all the way there. You had a good rest and the meeting is the next night. In the morning of the next day, you go all over Tokyo sight seeing. In the afternoon lunchtime, you had a large helping of Japanese delicacies for lunch.

Then you go and do all your shopping. Just about an hour before the meeting, you rush back into your hotel. You washed yourself quickly and go to the meeting. You may have ten volts but you may be able to flow only in about five volts of anointing since you have lowered your preparedness. You did not shut yourself aside to consecrate yourself to the Lord. See there is a price to pay in ministry.

Sometimes people do not realize the price you pay. I only share this with bible school students. Most of you want to know what goes on behind the scenes. Many people do not know I sleep very little on Saturday night. I get up early on Sunday morning and wait upon the Lord for the congregation. You pay the price. The sacrifices you made for the body. Sometimes when I travel if I minister, I consecrate myself onto the Lord.

My wife knows we do not have any sexual relationship at all when I minister. I just shut myself up onto the Lord. It is the price you pay and people sometimes do not appreciate the sacrifices you make. They do not realize the cause of pain behind the scene and the sacrifice you made. Praise God He will reward you in other ways.

We should realize that preparedness is necessary. By preparedness, I mean your personal relationship with God. There is a degree of preparedness. When I travel to places, I hardly go sightseeing. The only time I could do so is when the meeting is over.

Then I relax a little bit and I just let people take me around. A mission director told me how he took a group of foreigners to Singapore. He had this team of bible students. The moment the plane landed in Singapore, they started shopping. Everyone started discussing how to plan their shopping. They shopped till they dropped and they ended up suffering a series of misfortunes. Somebody lost his passport; some were delayed here and there.

Why, their minds were not on ministry. Preparedness affects the anointing of God in our life. If God calls you to minister in some way, God will expect you to give yourself. That is what we mean by giving yourself to your office and ministry. There are some things which I have said that those not in the ministry can never understand. Only those who have been in the ministry understand what is involved.

Those who have never lived by faith do not understand what is involved. Sometimes I feel grieved with people who are not in the ministry passing comments on those in the ministry. Wait until you get into it, and then you will realize what it is like.

A person who is successful in the world does not mean he will be successful in the ministry. It is a different thing altogether. Now the opposite is also true - a person who is successful in the ministry may not be successful in the world. The fact is that of all professions, the ministry has the highest price to pay.

It is easier to work in a secular job, give an encouraging word now and then to the pastor, and have a little home fellowship in your house. If you have never been in the ministry to give yourself to it, you do not understand the sacrifices that will be involved, the preparedness that is required and the sacrifices at home. For that reason Jesus in Jn. 17 says for this purpose, I sanctify Myself. He consecrated Himself because He has such a high mission for us. He gave Himself entirely to the Lord.

EXPECTANCY LEVEL

The third is the expectancy level that people have in our life that people have of you. Sometimes people will say it is just another meeting and the expectancy is not there. When the expectancy is there, you could operate at a higher level. Let us say that you operate at ten volts.

You go to a meeting where everybody did not really look forward to you operating in that anointing. In other words, the people did not pay a price to be ministered by you. Some people really pay a price to get ministered to. Some people will travel land, sea, and air to get ministered by you. Some people just lived next door and say, "

If I like it, I will be there. If I do not like it, I will not be there." There need to be a level of expectancy. One reason why sometimes the anointing works powerfully in some ministers' lives is because they are not so accessible. Let me give an example.

You only get to see the man of God in a meeting. He does not mix with the people. He does not talk much with the people. When it is time for him to minister, he shows up. When the ministering is ended, he goes off. You know what he does to the people.

Let me give both the positive and the negative point. There is a psychological factor being placed on the people. The people do not have easy access to the man of God. As a result, they look up to that person. As a result, they have a higher expectancy. They are not accessible.

You cannot go near to them and the people end up having higher expectations of him. It is very hard to get to them and the result is that the expectancy goes very high. This works as a plus and positive point for them. However, I do not see Jesus doing that. I do not recommend it to people. I would prefer to correct that kind of attitude. I am giving you the reason why some men of God do that.

They want to build people's expectancy of them. If you ever go to some of those big time ministries like in America, I tell you they have many bodyguards surrounding them. There is no way you could near to them. You could not even shake hands with them. They look so "special." As a result, you put them on a higher level and your expectancy goes up.

They are employing wrong methods but achieving right results. Jesus did not do that. He rather let it flow as it is. For that reason I have not done that and it is not my nature. My nature is to come to the level of people. Because of that, it can work against you sometimes.

This is how it can work against you. Some people do not know their limit with you. I mean you could be a friend with them, dine and drink together and joke together. So by the time you come to operate the anointing of God, they say, "

Ah, we are friends." They do not have any expectation of you because they say, "We know you." Some people know their limit but some do not know. In other words, some people could be close to you but they do not lose their respect for you. Some people are close to you and they take the opportunity to climb over your head. In the ministry, you got to relate wisely to people.

We have to relate to all people rich or poor, fat of thin and there are so many different personalities that we have to have the wisdom of God to know how to relate to each one. The most important thing I encourage is being close with the people of God and being one with them.

Sometimes I travel to meetings and the organizers tell me to make a grand entrance and secretly exit. I usually tell them I prefer to come and worship with the people. The people then know I am just one with them. However, when I move in the anointing that is when I am different from them.

I am ministering to them with the gift and the office of God. If they stand in their office and they minister like I Corinthians says that there could be two or three prophets in a meeting. If one prophet is ministering and has a word hear that person. However, if the word comes to another person, let the person sit down and let the other start speaking.

This is to create a body type of ministry. However, when we do it, people need to maintain a level of expectancy from the minister of God. For expectancy, people need to pay a price. If they do not pay a price, they do not have expectancy.

When they pay a price, they have expectancy. Just like the minister needs to prepare himself, the people also need to prepare themselves before a meeting. Instead of using wrong methods to heighten expectancy in the people, I would rather teach them to prepare themselves before they come to God. Then they can really receive whatever God has for their lives.

FIVE TYPES OF ANOINTING

The act of anointing signified consecration to a holy or sacred use; hence the anointing of the High Priest (Ex. 29:29; Lev. 4:3) and of the sacred vessels (Ex. 30:26). The HIGH PRIEST and the king are thus called "the anointed" (Lev. 4:3, 5, 16; 6:20; Ps. 132:10). Anointing a king was equivalent to crowning him (1 Sam. 16:13; 2 Sam. 2:4, etc.).Prophets were also anointed (1 Kings 19:16; 1 Chr. 16:22; Ps. 105:15). The expression, "anoint the shield" (Isa. 21:5), refers to the custom of rubbing oil on the leather of the shield to make it supple and suitable for use in war.

Anointing was also an act of hospitality (Luke 7:38, 46). It was the custom of the Jews to anoint themselves with oil, as a means of refreshing or invigorating their bodies (Deut. 28:40; Ruth 3:3; 2 Sam. 14:2; Ps. 104:15, etc.).Oil was used also for medicinal purposes. It was applied to the sick, and also to wounds (Ps. 109:18; Isa. 1:6; Mark 6:13; James 5:14).The bodies of the dead were sometimes anointed (Mark 14:8; Luke 23:56).The promised Deliverer is twice called the "Anointed" or Messiah (Ps. 2:2; Dan. 9:25-26), because he was anointed with the Holy Ghost (Isa. 61:1), figuratively the "oil of gladness" (Ps. 45:7; Heb. 1:9). Jesus of Nazareth is this anointed One (John 1:41; Acts 9:22; 17:2-3; 18:5, 28), the Messiah of the Old Testament.

Without the anointing, you cannot fulfill the work that God has given you to do. I do not think that any minister of the Word would disagree with me there. What you might not know, as one called as a prophet though, is that when the Lord called you to do His work, the anointing was part of the parcel that you received. Consider this passage:

Luke 4: 18 The Spirit of the Lord [is] upon me, because he has anointed me to preach the gospel to the poor; he has sent me to heal the brokenhearted, to preach deliverance to the captives, and recovering of sight to the blind, to set at liberty those that are bruised,

In other words, if the Lord has called you to do a work, He has given you the power that you need to fulfill it as well.I see so many praying for the anointing, as if it is something that the Lord would deliberately withhold from you.

You need to change your thinking. The anointing and your calling are a complete package.**Key Principle**: When the Lord called you, He gave you the anointing you needed to fulfill that call.When this principle sinks in, you can spend less time asking God to anoint you, and more time asking how to walk in His anointing by faith.Many have a strange idea about the anointing though.

They think of it as something that comes and goes. You imagine that the Lord anoints you just once, but then you must qualify for it again, and again.Well, to a certain extent, that was true in days gone by. Before Christ came - that is exactly what it was like when you needed the anointing.

The Holy Spirit descended on a great man of faith, and then left him once the work was done.Samson was a great example of this. The anointing would come upon him suddenly, and when that happened, he accomplished incredible feats.

Once the anointing left him though, he was weak once again.That is because Jesus had not yet died for our sins! Man was contaminated through sin. They had to sacrifice often to atone and "cover over" the sin in their lives.

And so a very righteous God could not reside with a very sinful man.I often wonder to myself how hard it must have been in those days. They had to keep the law using their will alone. They did not have the Holy Spirit within to make right choices. They had to wait for God to "come upon them" before they felt Him.No wonder the coming of Christ was such a mind-blowing change of thinking for the Early Church.

For the first time, the anointing came... and remained!1 John 2:27 But the anointing that you received from him remains in you, and you do not need anyone to teach you: but as the same anointing teaches you about all things, and is true, and is not a lie,

and just as it has taught you, you will abide in him.I love this passage. John tells us here, that the anointing that they received did not leave! It did not "come upon" and then "lift" from them again, and again.Instead of having to push through with pure willpower, they had a "big brother" in their corner by the name of the Holy Spirit.

For the first time ever, a righteous God could dwell within a sinful man – all because of the blood of Christ that washes away our sin.

When you understand this concept, you will not ask God again to "give you the anointing again" but you will ask Him to increase what you already have. You will ask Him for wisdom to use what is already in your spirit.

Then just as this scripture above says, that very anointing will teach you what you need to do to fulfill your purpose.In the next couple of chapters we are going to look at the New Testament prophet.

For it is the anointing that differentiates the Old from the New Testament prophet quite considerably.In the Old Testament, the prophet had to wait for God to suddenly come upon him before he could speak.

The same is not true of the New Testament prophet.Instead, when God calls and anoints you, He deposits that anointing right inside of your spirit.

That means you carry it with you everywhere you go. Now that does not mean that it is "your" anointing. It simply means that you have a reserve of power in your spirit that the Holy Spirit can use when He pleases.

He does not need to wait for you to be "righteous" according to the flesh, but He just needs to wait until you are available.Keep these simple principles in mind as we look in greater detail at what we now have in Christ.

You will learn that not only do we still have the external anointing just like they had in the Old Testament, but that we now have the internal anointing, which is depicted as streams of living water. This anointing is what sets you apart as a prophet. So let's teach you to tap into it, so that you can gush over the Church and bring it to life!

THE PROPHETIC ANOINTING

The first thing you need to know is that you already have the prophetic anointing. If God has called you to the prophetic ministry, you already have within you the anointing to get the job done. That is the easy part. You know, so many people are confused.

They think that they have to hop from conference to conference to get the prophetic anointing. No, you already have it. The part that is difficult is learning to identify it and then to flow in it correctly.

Defining the Anointing John 7:38 He that believes in me, out of his inward parts will flow rivers of living water. As a child I was really blessed. I grew up living near many recreational parks. My father, quite the adventurer, loved to take us out on weekends to visit these parks.

There was one in particular that he liked to take us to. With its rolling hills, it was the perfect place for some time alone. The best part of all though, was the meandering river that cut through the hills from one end to the other.

We would head out early, and spread our blanket out on the soft, fragrant grass. A picnic would follow with lots of goodies. After we were done, we would pack up, put all our stuff back in the car, and then we would go walking.

THE BUBBLING BROOK

We would find the river and follow it as much as we could. We would explore and see what there was to find: trees, stones, hidden ditches or bridges. It was fun to seek out the perfect skipping stone to send skimming over the water

.Even though this was years ago, just speaking about it, I can smell the fresh soil and the plant life next to the river. I can hear the sound of the water making a gentle chuckle as it flows over the rocks

.It is as real to me as if I went there yesterday. Each time I bring this memory to mind, it brings with it that familiar feeling of peace.The picture I painted is the perfect illustration of the prophetic anointing. It is like a gentle, bubbling brook that brings peace, joy and rest. It is not a mighty waterfall that comes splashing, picking you up and tossing you around.

No, that is the external anointing and that comes by the will of God alone.The prophetic anointing is something entirely different. It is a gentle bubbling that originates from deep within you. If you would jus stop for a moment, you would come to realize that you have been experiencing this for some time.

Perhaps you have been comparing yourself to other ministers and feeling a little insecure.

THE MIGHTY WATERFALL – THE EXTERNAL ANOINTING

You look at all these big revivalists and they bring a mighty outpouring of the Spirit. People talk about the "fire" and the "water," and people are getting slain in the spirit in their meetings. You see healings, miracles, shakings and a whole bunch of other stuff going on.

You take a step back and think, "Wow!"You compare yourself to them and when you look inside, you think, "Here I stand with just my little bubbling brook."

You know, I had the opportunity to go to the Rheinfall in Switzerland. It is the largest waterfall in Europe. It is absolutely magnificent.

The sound of the water is so loud that you have to shout at one another to be heard. It roars in your ears. A fine mist covers the whole river because of the intensity at which the water hits the lake with below.

It is incredible. I have been there a few times to visit, and each time has been wonderful, but I didn't spend hours there. You can only spend so long staring at a waterfall, and well... you have seen a waterfall. It is wonderful, it is magnificent and I take the experience home with me, but it is a place I have visited as a tourist only once or twice.

Waterfall vs. Brook

By comparison, as a child, when we went to the bubbling brook, I could sit there for hours just quietly taking in the sounds and smells. That sound refreshed my spirit. I could go back again, and again and never grow weary of it.It is great to have the great outpourings. We need them to be refreshed from time to time, but you can't live there.

TAPPING INTO THE ANOINTING

What you have is an anointing that people can take home with them. That when touched by it, continues to work within them. It is the kind of anointing that I spoke about in the introduction from 1 John 2:27. It is an anointing that abides.

You don't take a bucket of water and splash the water on their heads. Rather you are releasing a bubbling brook into their spirits.

You will bring the spirit inside of them to life! It is an anointing that will continue to bubble and flow like a beautiful spring that will come up and feed them again and again

What It Feels Like. So when you experience the anointing, realize that it is going to bubble from deep inside. I feel it right in the pit of my stomach. I feel it sometimes like butterflies. It is like the feeling you get the night before Christmas when you were hoping to get that "special something." You lay in bed at night and you were so excited.

Your stomach did flips and you couldn't sleep - you couldn't eat. Well, that's how I felt the night before I got married. I couldn't sleep the whole night. I was so excited and terrified all at the same time. That is what the internal anointing feels like. Now the first time that you experience it, it is probably going to be pretty strong.

Yes, there are many different manifestations of the anointing, but I am just just covering the prophetic anointing here. It may start very strong at the beginning, or perhaps very gentle. It will nudge you from deep within saying, "Hello, remember me? I am here, I want to tell you something." That's the Holy Spirit speaking inside of you.

HOW TO IDENTIFY IT

To hear that gentle voice you need to shut up. I know that you hear me telling you to do that a lot, but by the end of this series you will be used to me saying it. That is because as prophets, we either do not know how, or find it really hard to sit quietly instead of shouting our mouths off.

Key Principle: You need to learn to be quiet long enough to hear the voice of the Lord within. You will feel this anointing as a gentle stirring. The Holy Spirit is not going to run up to you, slap you on the side of the head and say, "Prophesy." It doesn't happen that wa.

He is going to gently remind you, and that reminder is going to come from deep down inside. You are not living in Old Testament times when the Lord had to wait for you to be righteous before He could come upon you. Now He can speak to you from within your spirit any time that He pleases. Your part in this conversation is to be silent long enough to hear Him.

HOW TO TAP INTO THE ANOINTING

How are you going to tap into it? We know we have this river of living water inside of us, and sometimes you even feel it. Now, what do you do with it? You need to realize that releasing this anointing is very much the same as journaling. I have already taken you through the whole process of decreeing, and journaling in the Prophetic Functions book. I will also teach you about intercession later on in this book. So, by now you should be familiar with the stirring you feel inside your belly. When you start to journal it feels slow, but the more you write, the easier it gets. The anointing starts to flow and the words flow faster than you can type - faster than you can speak. You feel that bubbling coming up inside of you.

Well, that is the prophetic anointing that you have been experiencing! You have been experiencing it all along. Now you need to learn to use it when ministering.

1. MAKE YOURSELF AVAILABLE

The first thing you need to do is make yourself available. Say now, you are in a meeting, or somebody comes to you for prayer. You can only say,

"Lord, I am a vessel. I have got your living waters inside of me. I open up my mouth and it is for you to fill it."

Key Principle: You tap into the anointing by making yourself available, desiring to be used by the Lord, and by stepping out in faith.

2. FAITH IS THE KEY

You can learn to flow in the spirit this way. Once you identify the river of living water inside of you, you can trigger it by faith at any time. If I make a conscious effort to stop and tap into the anointing, I can release that anointing any time I desire, because I am a prophet.

Now keep in mind that I am speaking about the anointing here, and not the gifts of the Spirit! The gifts are only manifested by the Holy Spirit. However, when those gifts do manifest, if you act in faith, the anointing will follow.

Key Principle:

The gifts: manifested as the Holy Spirit wills. The anointing that brings the revelation to pass: released by your faith.

When you reach prophetic office, you are going to realize that the anointing is available to you at any time.

3. IT REMAINS IN YOUR SPIRIT.

There are times though when people come to you and you need to tap into that anointing fast.

People sometimes need ministry at the most inconvenient times! The doorbell rings, and you just had a fight with your spouse, the house is a mess, you messed up at work that day, you stubbed your toe, and then tripped over the dog on your way to answer the door.

There, standing in front of you, is someone saying, "Please could you pray for me?"

With an incredulous intake of breath, you think, "Are you kidding me, Lord? The last thing I feel right now is your power. I had a horrible day, and I don't feel very spiritual at all at the moment."Well then, just as well, the anointing is not dependent on you, hey?

Thank goodness it depends on the Holy Spirit.Definition of "Anoint" and "Anointed" in the Bible"Anoint" and "anointing" are critical to understand terms in biblical terminology. For people in many places today, especially modern and/or western societies, the meaning of those words and what they involved in biblical times is not immediately perceived. Not without an explanation.

In order to fully grasp the meaning of such words, however, the explanation must be both comprehensive as well as simple. Such balance between comprehensiveness and simplicity, despite not always being easy to achieve, is what this article is intended for - and aims at. After all, what those words involve, at least to a degree, is so profound that it can greatly impact anyone's life - including yours.

In order to achieve the aforementioned comprehensiveness and simplicity, let us "divide" the explanation into the different applications the word has in the Bible:

(1) the use of such word when referring to certain customs and practices of the day-to-day life of ancient Israelites and other Middle Eastern nations, and

(3) its use regarding spiritual matters and God's purpose for humans and the earth. Before going into such explanation, however, it is fundamental to first understand the basic meaning of "anoint"/"anointed" as used in the Bible. Here is a simple definition:

(4) TheHebrew sukh and the Greek a·lei′ phoare the words used in the Bible for "anoint" or "anointing". Their basic meaning refers to **the commonplace greasing, or rubbing on of oil.** (Daniel 10:3; Ruth 3:3; John 11:2) But for a special anointing with oil, the Bible generally uses the Hebrew word ma·shach′ , from which the wordma·shi′ ach(Messiah) comes,

(5) and the Greek word khri′o, from which comeskhri·stos′ (Christ). (Exodus 30:30; Leviticus 4:5; Luke 4:18; Acts 4:26) This distinction is maintained quite consistently both in the Hebrew and in the Greek. Some versions of the Bible do not maintain this fine distinction, but translate all such words by the one term "anoint."

(6) Therefore, in ancient times, the Israelites and other nations around easily understood that "anoint" or "anointing", in its common use, **referred to the process of greasing with oil.** In simple terms, that is the basic meaning of those terms.

Nonetheless, as mentioned above, such greasing with oil could have two very different uses: the common use (related with point (1), in the previous paragraph) and a special use, that is, a special type of anointing (related with point (2) in the previous paragraph). Let us start with its common use, that is, its use regarding certain customs and practices of the day-to-day life of the people of Biblical times, especially the Israelites of old.

COSTLY PERFUMES IN EARLY TIMES

In the days of the kings of Israel, the rich used perfumes to give fragrance to their houses, garments, and couches. Perfumers in ancient times even formed trade groups. (Nehemiah 3:8; Psalm 45:8; Song of Solomon 3:6, 7)

The genuine nard that Mary, sister of Lazarus, used to anoint Jesus' feet was worth nearly a farm worker's wages for a year. (John 12:3-5) Yes, costly perfumes have been in use since early times!Anointing –

It's Different Meanings In The Daily Life of Old.Although for people in many places today the meaning of "anoint" and "anointing" is not immediately perceived without an explanation, for people of ancient times described in the Bible, and even for many societies nowadays, the meaning of such words was/is neither obscure nor hard to understand. Two reasons for that are habits of life and culture. In the lands of the Middle East

, it was a common practice in old times to rub oil on the body. Such oil was, generally, olive oil (very common in those lands) to which they would add perfume. Rubbing the body with oil (literally, anointing the body), normally applied after bathing, was very helpful in protecting the exposed parts of the body against the effects of the intense rays of the sun.

Another benefit of the practice of rubbing the body with oil (literally, anointing the body) was that the oil also helped to keep the skin supple.

That was yet another reason for Israelites, and others, to "anoint" their bodies, that is, to rub them with oil. Since the Bible often describes daily life practices and activities of Israelites, like the custom of rubbing oil on the body, such use of the verb to "anoint" is not uncommon.

The following are some Biblical examples of just that.A Sneak peek Into History.In the year 1117 B.C.E. God authorized Samuel to anoint Saul the son of Kish of the tribe of Benjamin to be king over all Israel. Being anointed as king by God's prophet,

Saul became "the anointed of Jehovah." – 1 Samuel 12:3, 5; 24:6, 10.Biblical ExamplesThe Bible tells us about an Israelite young woman who came to be chosen be a mighty king, King Ahasuerus, to be his wife and queen. Before been presented to the king, however, this beautiful young woman, Esther, underwent a course of massage treatment for six months with oil of myrrh and with oil of balsam before being presented to King Ahasuerus

. We can read this in the Bible in the book of Esther, chapter 2 and verse 12 (Esther 2:12). Now, if we were reading this in the original language, we would read that Esther underwent a treatment of "anointing" her body with myrrh and balsam for six months, together with massages.Another example of this common use of "anoint" can be found in Mark 14:8 andLuke 23:56.

There is described the common practice of greasing the body of someone who had just died with oil (that is, anointing it), as a preparation for the burial.

That was done both as a sign of respect, as well as to supple the skin in order for it to maintain its elasticity and to not start the decomposing process as fast (the customary heat of such lands would accelerate the start of decomposing).

Yet another example of this common practice in daily life is shown by an event related to Jesus himself. As Jesus indicated in his words regarding the woman who greased his feet with perfumed oil, to grease the head or, as in this case, the feet of a guest with oil was regarded as an act of hospitality and courtesy. (Luke 7:38, 46).

Many other examples could be given, but the ones provided above are sufficient to understand that one of the meanings of "anointing" in the Bible is related to daily, literal, activities of the people. And that there was no special meaning related to such customary, daily practices.

However, there was/is a much more important type of "anointing" in the Bible - a special type of anointing. Its meaning went far beyond the literal greasing of some part of the body with oil. In this special type of anointing, the most important was not the act of greasing itself, but the symbolicmeaning of such greasing with oil. That is what we shall discuss now

.Anointed Without Oil - How So?There are instances in which a person was regarded as being anointed because of being appointed by God, even though no oil was put on his head. Among others, a Biblical example which proves that is the Persian king Cyrus, whom Isaiah had foretold that Jehovah would use as His anointed. (Isaiah 45:1)

Cyrus was not actually anointed with oil by one of Jehovah's representatives, but because he was appointed by Jehovah to do a certain work, he could be said to be anointed.Anointing - Its Symbolic and Most Important Meaning.The Bible also often refers to a different type of anointing - a special type. Not that it didn't involve greasing with oil. It did. But the meaning of such greasing with oil was far more special because of what it meant.

So different - in its meaning - was this type of anointing from the normal greasing with oil (that anyone could do) that even a different word was used to refer to such "anointing". In Hebrew such word was ma·shach´ (for the normal "anoint" described above in this article, the word used was sukh), from which the word ma·shi´ ach(Messiah) comes, and in Greek the word was khri´ o, from which comeskhri·stos´ (Christ).

This type of "anointing" was so special that, not only was it referred to by different words, but even a completely special oil - specifically made for such special "anointing" (greasing) - was used. The question, then, is: what was so special about that type of anointing?

The answer?In simple terms, because of its significance/meaning. Being someone greased, or anointed, with such special oil was a **confirmation of their official appointment to office**. During the times of Biblical history, both the Hebrews (Israelites) and some of the non-Hebrews ceremonially anointed rulers.

Nonetheless, when Jehovah (Jehovah is the name of God in the Bible), **God, appointed someone to do a certain work, or to an office**, like king, he would order a prophet to take the special oil and "anoint" such a person, that is, grease him with oil.

That special anointing was the confirmation of their appointment by God. When a person was anointed with such oil, the oil was put on his head and allowed to run down onto his beard and onto the collar of his garments. (Psalms 133:2)

Here are some Biblical examples of such special anointing:Samuel anointed Saul as king after God had designated Saul as his choice. (1Samuel 10:1) David was anointed as king on three different occasions: once by Samuel, later by the men of Judah and finally by all the tribes. (1Samuel 16:13; 2Samuel 2:4; 5:3)

Aaron was anointed after his appointment to the office of high priest. (Leviticus 8:12) Afterward, Aaron and his sons had some of the anointing oil, along with the blood of the sacrifices, splattered upon their garments, but Aaron was the only one who had the oil poured over his head. -- Leviticus 8:30

A SPECIAL OIL

In the Law Jehovah gave to Moses, he prescribed a formula for the anointing oil. It was of a special composition of the choicest ingredients--myrrh, sweet cinnamon, sweet calamus, cassia, and olive oil. (Exodus 30:22-25)

It was a capital offense for anyone to compound this mixture and to use it for any common or unauthorized purpose. (Exodus 30:31-33)

This figuratively demonstrated the importance and sacredness of an appointment to office that had been confirmed by anointing with sacred oil. If an appointment to office by means of an oil was so important, one made by means of anointing with holy spirit would be much more sacred, official and important!

AN EVEN GREATER TYPE OF ANOINTING

Although many men were anointed, or appointed, to a special work or office, there is one of such anointed ones that is referred to in special terms and with special honor. He was spoken of even before he came into existence as a human and many prophecies were written to provide details about such special person, who would be superior to all other anointed before and after him.

Even a date for his appearance as the Anointed One, the Leader, was provided by means of a spectacular prophecy written centuries before its actual fulfillment. You can read such prophecy in Daniel 9:25, 26. Hundreds of prophecies were written ahead of time to provide different details about this Anointed One.

Guiding themselves by the prophecy in Daniel 9:25, 26 the Jews of the first century CE (Common Era) in general were expecting the Messiah, the Anointed One. Who would he be?Fulfilling many prophecies in the Hebrew Scriptures, Jesus of Nazareth proved to be the Anointed One of Jehovah and could properly be called Messiah, or Christ, which titles convey that thought. (Matthew 1:16; Hebrews 1:8, 9)

His anointing, however, was far better and grander than that of any other man that lived before him. In what sense?Instead of being anointed with literal oil, he was anointed with Jehovah's holy spirit. (Matthew 3:16)

This was Jehovah's appointment of him as King, Prophet, and High Priest, and so he was referred to as Jehovah's Anointed. (Psalms 2:2; Acts 3:20-26; 4:26, 27; Hebrews 5:5, 6) Jesus Christ is the only one in the Scriptures who holds an anointing to all three offices: prophet, high priest, and king.

Additionally, his anointing was far superior also because of certain superior factors involved in his anointing. For example, although men prior to him were anointed for an office, by commandment of God, such anointing would be by means of a prophet, that is, another human who would pour the special oil on his head.

In Jesus case, God did not send any man to anoint Jesus, but He did it himself, personally, from heaven. Therefore, Jesus received his anointing directly from Jehovah, the Almighty, himself, not by means of a human. Another reason why Jesus anointing was superior was that he was anointed not with oil, like all those before him, but with holy spirit. And his anointing, or appointing to office, was not for an earthly kingship, but to a heavenly one and not only to be King, but also to the office of heavenly High Priest. (Hebrews 1:9; Psalms 45:7) What does all that mean?

WHAT IS A GOVERNMENT

A kingdom is a form of government like democracy is a form of government. And the government are the peoplethat are in office, that were appointedto govern over the rest of the nation.

Together, the people in such offices form a government.What Does It All Mean?By thus appointing, or commissioning, Jesus, that is, by anointing him in such a manner (personally and with holy spirit) to a heavenly kingship

, God himself bore witness that Jesus was the one He personally chose to fulfill, among many others, the prophecies inGenesis 49:10 and Isaiah 11:1, 2, 10about his Kingdom (God's kingdom).

Jesus, thus, became the undisputed and sole owner of the right to be King, in heaven, over the earth

. In this way, it is possible to start to understand a little of the profound meaning of the Lord's Prayer when it says, in part: "your kingdom come, your will be done, on earth as in heaven" (Matthew 6:10 - New Jerusalem Bible) What is this Kingdom and how does God's Kingdom relate to Jesus anointing with holy spirit when he was 30 years old? Well, a kingdom is a form of government, like democracy is a form of government.

When, thus, we refer to a kingdom we are referring not to the land, to the borders of a country or to the people that constitute a nation, but to the government of that country. And the government are the people that are in office, that were appointedto govern over the rest of the nation.

For example, the government of Portugal refers to the Prime Minister and to the ministers he appoints to the different areas of government (Internal Affairs, Department of Treasury, Department of Defense, and so forth).

Together, the people in such offices **are** the Government of Portugal. In like manner, by appointing Jesus as King, when anointing him with holy spirit at the time of his baptism, God started to form His Kingdom –

that is, the group of people He chose to govern – of which Jesus, His own son, is the King (or Prime Minister).* But is God's Kingdom, or God's Government, formed by only one person - Jesus? And where is the capital of God's Kingdom?

ONE WORLD,ONE GOVERNMENT

ounselors and advisers on world affairs are continually being frustrated. Whether they like the thought or not, they are being forced to the conclusion that the human family is unable to govern itself. It has not by itself brought forth the type of government that has made or can make all mankind one world.A Kingdom of How Many Anointed Ones?

Lets us start with where is the capital of God's Kingdom, that is, from where will God's Kingdom rule. Well, where is Jesus? You will remember that Jesus was put to death on a torture stake at the age of 33, and then he was resurrected. Shortly thereafter, he ascended to heaven. (Acts 2:33)

Hence, that is where God's Kingdom capital is -- in heaven. That is why the Bible calls it a "heavenly kingdom." (2 Timothy 4:18) Although God's Kingdom is in heaven, it will rule over the entire earth. –

Revelation 11:15.As for the question "is God's Kingdom, or God's Government, formed by only one person - Jesus?" the answer is "No". He will have co-rulers. For example, the apostle Paul told Timothy:

"If we go on enduring, we shall also rule together as kings." (Italics mine) (2 Timothy 2:12) Yes, Paul, Timothy, and other faithful ones who have been selected by God were also anointed with holy spirit and will rule together with Jesus in heaven – forming a heavenly Kingdom.

That means that, as Jesus, those who were also anointed, or appointed, by God to be kings with Christ* will have to go to heaven. How many will have that privilege?

A COMPARISON

Comparing God's Kingdom to some democratic structures of government, as Portugal, for example, Jehovah, Jesus' Father, could be compared to the President of the Republic. The President of the Republic is not part of the government, but is above the government and can dismiss the government should the circumstances so demand.

In like manner, God is notpart of His Kingdom, but is above such Kingdom and is greater than the Kingdom. Nonetheless, the Kingdom is referred to as God's Kingdom because it is God who personally appoints, oranoints all people that form such government, or Kingdom.

A SPECIFIC NUMBER OR ALL GOOD PEOPLE?

The last book of the Bible, Revelation, discloses that to us nicely. It describes "the Lamb [Jesus Christ*] standing upon Mount Zion [his royal position in heaven], and with him a hundred and forty-four thousand having his name and the name of his Father written on their foreheads." (Revelation 14:1) (Italics mine) Who are those 144,000?The answer is three verses below, when it says: "These are the ones that keep following the Lamb no matter where he goes.

These werebought from among mankind as firstfruits to God and to the Lamb." (Italics mine) (Revelation 14:4) Yes, they are not angels, but faithful followers of Jesus Christ especially chosen from the earth to rule in heaven with him. Together, Jesus (as King, or Prime Minister, so to speak) and the 144,000 (like helping ministers) **are/form** God's Kingdom. After being raised from death to heavenly life, the 144,000 "are to rule as kings over the earth" along with Jesus.

(Revelation 5:10) Since the days of the apostles, God has been selecting faithful Christians in order to complete the number 144,000.

And that is the **total number**of humans that go to heaven. What then, will happen to all the other good people?A government, or kingdom, is only needed while there are people to govern over. Logically, there would be no need for God to set a government, or kingdom, in place to rule over the earth if there were no people on earth to rule over. That is why Jesus himself, while still on earth, clearly revealed: "Blessed are the meek for they shall inherit the **earth**." (Bold mine) (Matthew 5:5 -- King James Bible).

Therefore, Jesus and the 144,00 appointed by God to form his Kingdom shall rule over those who qualify to be subjects, on earth, of God's Kingdom.

But here is a question for you: The Lord's Prayer also says: "your kingdom come, your will be done, on earth as in heaven". (Italics mine)

Accordingly, what is God's will for the "earth" and how will it be done? And how can you benefit? That will be the topic of a future article.

Bottom of Form

CARRIERS OF GOD'S ANOINTING

INTRODUCTION

Many books had been written on the "anointing." This generation is a blessed one. Knowledge is being increased both in secular and spiritual realms.Nevertheless, I have met many people boasting about the anointing, but only a few who really walk in the anointing.Fourteen years as a disciple of Jesus, I am still learning, longing and yearning to continuously walk in the anointing.

One thing I have learned is that in order to walk in th anointing there is a price to pay, and it is not cheap. It is something to receive the anointing and another thing to walk in it. I pray that through this book, my best friend, the Holy Spirit will enable me to help those who have decided to pay the price. Otherwise, they will just have read another book. [All scripture references are from the NKJV unless otherwise noted.]

THE ANOINTING

Firstly, what does it mean to anoint, the anointing or to be anointed? There are many Hebrew and Greek words in relation to anointing. But for the sake of study, I will only mention a few.

The Basic meaning of the word anoint is simply to smear something on an object. Usually oil is involved, but it could be other substances such as paint or dye. This gives the idea that to anoint something or someone is an act of consecration.Mashyach: 'anointed one' one who is consecrated for a special office or function.In simple terms, the anointing is the presence of the Holy Spirit being smeared upon someone.

It is the overflowing life of Jesus which imparts supernatural strength enabling an individual to perform a special task or function in an office he is called and appointed to.In ancient times, God would anoint an individual to function effectively to a particular office. For example,

He would choose a person and anoint him to stand in the office of a prophet. He would choose another and anoint him to stand in the office of a priest. He would choose still another one and anoint him to stand in the office of a king.David, God's chosen one, had the anointing of a king, a prophet and 2 Samuel 24:25These office were also combined in Christ the Messiah and for the spirit-filled church.Jesus our model.When you study about the life of Jesus, it is not a secret that when He was here on earth, He walked in the anointing.

When He became incarnate, He emptied Himself of the glory that He had with the Father before the foundation of the world as the pre-incarnate word of God. The glory of being equal with the Father in the gospel of Matthew chapter 3, Jesus came to John the Baptist at the Jordan river to be baptized by him. When He had been baptized, the heavens were opened to Him, and

He waw the spirit of God descending like a dove by the Holy Spirit into the wilderness to be tempted by the devil. Soon after, Jesus won the first round and started Him ministry with the anointing.In Luke 4:18, 19, He said,The spirit of the Lord is upon me because He has anointed me to preach the gospel to the poor;

He has sent me to heal the brokenhearted; Tp proclaim liberty to the captives and recovery of sight to the blind, To set at liberty those who are oppressed;To proclaim the acceptable year of the Lord.You can see what the anointing of God can do in the life of an individual who is called by God.

After the wilderness experience, Jesus did not remain passive, but He started to demonstrate the power of God's kingdom in destroying the works of the devil. The anointing is for service to the King of kings. It is not to build our little kingdoms on earth.

Jesus was there to do God's will, not to please an organization, nor man but to be the carrier of God's anointing.There is no power, no atomic bomb, and no technology that can destroy the works of the enemy of our souls

. It is only the anointing of El Shaddai that can break the yokes.It shall come to pass in that day that his burden will be taken away from your shoulder, and his yoke from your neck, and the yoke will be destroyed because of the anointing oil. Isaiah 10:27.If Jesus needed to be anointed on earth, we need also to be anointed, otherwise we will be no match for the devil.

KNOWN IN HELL

In the book of Acts chapter 19, we have an account where Paul was in Ephesus speaking about the Holy Spirit. He was full of the anointing where God worked unusual miracles by his hands so that handkerchiefs and aprons were brought from his body to the sick, and the diseases left them and the evil spirit went out of them.

There were some imitators who were not called by God and, without the anointing, who tried

TO CAST OUT EVIL SPIRITS.

And the evil spirit answered, Jesus I know, and Paul I know, but who are you? Acts 19:15Jesus was known and is known in Hell. Paul also was known in Hell. The anointing was so strong upon them the evil spirit seems to say:"When these guys awake every morning,

It makes hell tremble. But you, who are you?"Then the man in whom the evil spirit was, leaped on them, overpowered them, and prevailed against them, so that they fled out of that house naked and wounded.Acts 19:16These people were trying to merchandise the anointing. Satan is not a creator. He is a duplicator and a counterfeiter

. He always tries to imitate the genuine, right in the midst of many Christian gatherings. He administrates imitations. Now please don't misunderstand. These are genuine moves of the Holy Spirit, but in these last days we must discern, having the eyes of our spirit enlightened to detect the imitation from the genuine. We must not take everything for granted. Those who are really anointed will bring life to others.

THE SPIRIT OF KORAH

In Numbers, chapter 16, there was a man named Korah, a Levite. This man had a hidden agenda. He was inspired by the devil and caused 250 leaders of the congregation to contend and rebel against God's instituted authority figures - Moses and Aaron. Korah was jealous and wanted to win the priesthood for himself and his associates. We know about their end. They lost their lives.

Then in Numbers, chapter 17, God spoke to Moses and told him to get a rod from each tribe leader (twelve in all). The name of each leader should be written on each rod. Particularly, Aaron's name was to be written on his rod....the rod of the man whom I choose will blossom;Numbers 17:4-5Now it came to pass on the next day, that Moses went into the tabernacle of witness, and behold, the rod of Aaron, of the house of Levi, had sprouted and put forth buds, had produced blossoms, and yielded ripe almonds.

Numbers 17:8God said in verse 10, that it will be a sign against the rebels.God put life in the rod of Aaron. Aaron was a ministry of life. If you are sitting under a ministry where you are dying, get out before it is too late. Anyone called by God and anointed must be a life-giver.Paul said in I Corinthians 2:4:And my speech and my preaching were not with persuasive words of human wisdom, but in demonstration of the Spirit and of power.Oil,

A Symbol of the Holy Spirit.The word "symbol" is made up of two Greek words. Sym which means "together", and ballein, which means "to throw."Both words "thrown together" denotes an object used to represent something else. An emblem is the use of one thing to represent another. Therefore, oil is a symbol of the Holy Spirit because of some proper characteristics.

Now, let us have a look in the book of Exodus chapter 30 and let the Holy Spirit give us insight to understand more in the realm of anointing.

Moreover the Lord spoke to Moses saying, Also take for yourself quality spices - five hundred shekels of liquid myrrh, half as much sweet smelling cinnamon (two hundred and fifty shekels), two hundred and fifty of sweet smelling cane. Five hundred shekels of cassia, according to the shekel of sanctuary and a him of olive oil.

And you shall make from these a holy anointing oil, an ointment compounded according to the art of the perfumer. It shall be a holy anointing oil.Exodus 30:22-25,First mentioned are the spices and their appropriate weight.

The spices which were to be used must be of quality (NKJV) or principal (KJV). It is from the Hebrew word roshemeaning - the head, the chief, the first, or excellent.God instructed Moses to use the best spices as ingredients of the anointing oil. They were valuable, costly and rare.

They were not common or cheap.There were four spices plus a hin of olive oil that were to be used Myrrh ,Cinnamon ,Calamus (or cane)Cassia and olive oil.The number "5" in the Bible speaks of GRACE.

Grace means FAVOUR. God knows that man had become a weak creature after the fall and he is no match for the devil. Therefore, He yearns to supply us by His Spirit the anointing, to favour

His children with His ability and strength to re-enforce Jesus' victory on Calvary.Now, let's describe each spice and its spiritual application.Myrrh,Myrrh is a pale yellow gummy substance or liquid from a small thorny shrub which grows in Somalia, Ethiopia and Arabia.

It is used for spice or as an ointment. The best of it flows freely without the act of man. The oil of myrrh is purifying in its application. It is very costly.

Fragrant at the smell and bitter to the taste. It is also used as a balm to rub on sore parts of the body to bring relief.

So, the person of the Holy Spirit is a gift given by the grace of God to the body of Christ. He cannot be purchased because He is priceless. He shall never be addressed as "it", because He is God and needs to be obeyed and worshiped.The first thing He wants to do in an individual so that person can be used as a vessel of honor is to bring the spiritual myrrh to purify the vessel....

He will baptize you with the Holy Spirit and fire.Matthew 3:11The fire of the Holy Spirit is not for our destruction, but for our purification - to render us fit for the Master's use.If a man therefore purge himself from these, he shall be a vessel unto honour, sanctified, and meet for the Master's use, and prepared unto every good work.II Timothy 2:21Though we go through the fire of purification, the Holy Spirit is our Comforter.

When someone goes through this process, he sometimes endures some pain. But the Comforter rubs His sweet presence on the aching parts to bring relief.If you want to be used by God, my dear brothers and sister, let the fire of the Holy Spirit come and burn all the straws (which are impurities of the flesh).

Sure, the experience of purification is bitter, but in the end we will be a sweet fragrance in the nostrils of our Beloved Father. Therefore, myrrh speaks of purification.Cinnamon,The cinnamon oil is distilled from the bark of the cinnamon tree growing in Ceylon.

It is something very tasty and is usually used to flavor food because of its pleasant aroma.God said to Israel in Leviticus 26:31, "I will not smell the fragrance of your sweet aromas." Because of the disobedience of Israel, whatever they were offering or doing for God's satisfaction was not pleasant to Him. Whenever God's children are disobedient to Him, He is not pleased with their prayers or whatever sacrifice they can offer to Him. God cannot be bribed.

To obey is better than sacrifice.I Samuel 15:22,In the book of Ecclesiastes chapter 5, God addressed these as fools who offer a sacrifice to Him but were not obedient to Him. I know of many precious servants of God (called by God) who can be powerful instruments in the hands of God Almighty, but they remain stagnant and unfruitful.

They are satisfied with what is good, and they don't go for the best. Why? It is because they have chosen rather to obey man and man-made traditions other than God. To obey God there is a price to pay, and it's not cheap.You will have to let go of many things which you have put your trust in.

You will lose many so-called "friends." You are their friends as long as you stay in "their" church. When you leave, you become their "enemy." At a certain time in your life and having paid the price, you will feel yourself lonely, misunderstood and rejected by someone. This is the cost of the sweet spiritual cinnamon, but in the end it will pay off.It is at this very moment that the blending process by the master apothecary starts. He will be your real partner and will bring genuine and faithful friends to your side. Then your life will be tasteful and a pleasant aroma unto God.

The cinnamon speaks of obedience.Calamus (or cane),The calamus is a sweet cane plant of about ten feet high growing in Asia in marshy places. When it is crushed and broken, it exudes a sweet fragrance. The more it is broken, more of the fragrance is exuded.

In its spiritual application, the calamus speaks of brokenness.But on this one will I look on him who is poor and oaf a contrite spirit, and who trembles at my word.Isaiah 66:2,The word contrite in Hebrew is "nakeh" meaning smitten.

A second word "dakah" meaning to crumble, to bruise, to break into pieces. Now the word to refer in Hebrew is "nabat" - meaning to to regard with pleasure, to favour, to care, to consider and to have respect.When you study the book of Mark, chapter 14,

you can learn a valuable lesson concerning brokenness. Many precious friends in the service of the Lord are battling to walk in the anointing in a high level, but find themselves at the same measure they started. It is because they have not passed from the brokenness stage.

Therefore, an ingredient is missing in their lives.In the book of Mark, there was a certain woman who came into the house of Simon, the leper, where Jesus was in Bethany. This woman was in possession of a very precious thing - an alabaster flask of spikenard. It is a very expensive and rare substance extracted from a variety of bearded grass growing in India.

This flask of spikenard had cost the woman about three hundred days of labor. How many years might this woman have worked to save money to buy it when some merchants came to her village, maybe once a year? She bought some this year, some next year and so on.

When the flask was filled, she sealed it and kept it to anoint her bridegroom on the day of their wedding. But the Bible says that she broke the flask, her life of sacrifice, and poured the spikenard on the head of Jesus

The people were mad at her. She gave to Jesus the most precious and valuable thing that a woman could possess and reserve for her husband-to-be.For the perfume to be exuded, the flask had to be broken.

For the Calamus to exude its sweet fragrance, it must be bruised and broken. For one's life to be pleasurable and acceptable to be God's carrier of His anointing, one must be broken.The Calamus must always stand erect in muddy waters.It speaks about pride.Pride can prevent you from experiencing brokenness.

As long as a person keeps pride, he cannot carry a high level of the anointing in his life. We used to say, "Hey, have you noticed how many people I have in my church. How much money I have in the bank. The car I am driving. I don't preach to small churches. I preach only in big ones.

I don't submit to anyone sir, I am the authority." We must change that kind of attitude. It is pride sir, I call it by its name. Get rid of pride, or you will stop the flow of God's anointing in your life.God says in His word that He will consider, have pleasure and respect favorably him who has been broken.For it seems to me that God has made an exhibit of us Apostles, exposing us to view last [of all, like men in triumphal procession who are] sentenced to death [and displayed at the end of the line]. For we have become a spectacle to the world - a show in the world's amphitheater - with both men and angels [as spectators].We are [looked upon as] fools on account of Christ and for His sake, but you are [supposedly] so amazingly wise and prudent in Christ! We are weak but you are [so very] strong!

You are highly esteemed, but we are in disrepute and contempt!To this hour we have gone both hungry and thirsty, we habitually wear but one undergarment [and shiver in the cold]; we are roughly knocked about and wander around homeless.And we still toil unto weariness [for our living] working hard with our own hands. When men revile us, that is, wound us with an accursed sting - we bless them.

When we are persecuted, we take it patiently and endure it.When we are slandered and defamed, we [try to] answer softly and bring comfort. We have been made and are now the rubbish and filth of the world. The offscouring of all things, the scum of the earth.I Corinthians 4:9-13 (amplified version).In other words, Paul said

, "We have lost our reputation. We have not the approval of man. We have been broken."But God is saying, "You who have lost your reputation. You who have been broken. You who are not approved by man. I, God, am taking over. You now have approval.

My anointing over your life is My approval. I am regarding you with pleasure. I respect you, and I will continuously bestow my favour upon you."CassiaCassia is the aromatic bark of a tree growing in Arabia. It is often used by some doctors as medicine. Cassia is derived from a Hebrew root word - quadad meaning to bend, to bow, or to stoop.Bow down, then, before the strong hand of God.

He will raise you up, when His time to deliver you comes.1 Peter 5:6 (Knox translation)Cassia speaks of humility.Pride is not an influence. It is a demon spirit trying to destroy the life of the people of God. Earlier when I wrote on Calamus, I spoke briefly on pride. But in this part of study, we will go a step further.Over all the pride of earth,

he reigns supreme.Job4:34 (Knox translation)When you study this chapter of Job, you will notice that the writer was speaking about Leviathan. It is said that he reigns supreme over all the pride of the earth. Then all who are tolerating pride in their lives are making Leviathan their master.

The man who hopes to master him will be disillusioned; at the sight of him a person is paralyzed.Job 4:9 (Berkeley version)Leviathan is paralyzing homes, businesses and ministries etc. Through pride, it is stopping the flow of life and brining stagnancy. No human being can master the king of pride.

When roused, he grows ferocious, no one can face him in a fight.Job 41:10 (Jerusalem version).Leviathan means a wreathed animal such as a serpent, a crocodile or a large sea monster. It speaks about satan himself, wreathed with the scales of pride. (Job 41:15).

When one is anointed, he is rubbed with the very presence of God. But when one allows pride in his heart, he is "rubbed" with the scales of Leviathan which are:Pride - unduly high opinions of one's own qualities or merits.Arrogance - overbearance through an exaggerated feeling of one's superiority.

Contention - an assertion made in arguing.Boasting - speaking of oneself in such a manner to impress people.Haughty - proud of oneself and looking down on others.Witchcraft - misuse of spiritual power to control others.Control - the power of restraint.Manipulation - to influence craftily in order to cause others to wuit one's purpose.Domination –

to have a commanding or controlling influence over.Rebellion - refusing allegiance to an established government, open resistance to righteousness authority.Stubbornness - not easy to deal with.

Stubbornness leads to rebellion, rebellion leads to pride and pride leads to destruction.Submission is the path to humility and humility is that path to promotion. A continuous walk in humility will cause a double portion of God's anointing to flow in an individual's life.

Strength has made a home in his neck, fear leaps before him as he goes.Job 41:22 (Jerusalem version)Fear is a companion of pride. One who is prideful also has fear in his life. One who leans totally upon the Lord is not afraid.For I know thy rebellion and thy stiff-necked.

Deuteronomy 3:27.The strength of Leviathan resides in its neck. When someone is stubborn (stiff-necked) satan controls his strength, and the flow of God's anointing in his life commences to be dry.

If someone has grey areas in his life, God will speak to him many times for him to make readjustment and to repent. If this person disobeys and becomes stiff-necked, it will lead him to rebellion.

Then the door will be opened for Leviathan to wow the seed of pride. When pride's seed is fully grown, the scales will start to grow, then destruction will begin.I have pursued my enemies and overtaken them, neither did I turn back again till they were destroyed

.I have wounded them so that they could not rise, they have fallen under my feet.For you have armed me with strength for the battle, you have subdued under me those who rose up against me.You have also given me the necks of my enemies...Psalms 18:37-40.God has given to us the neck of Leviathan. When we walk in humility, we will walk in the anointing and the yoke will be broken in our lives.

Olive OilThe olive oil was one of the main tree crops of ancient Israel. It was during the month of November that the olives were picked and pressed for oil.Olive trees can stand for long periods of drought. They take two years to mature, and then the fruits ripen slowly.

The olives are placed on a grooved stone wheel and another stone is turned over them which is worked by a beam. The pulp is then pressed under weight.

The oil runs into stone vats where it is then left for sometime to settle and clear.Then was Jesus led up of the Spirit into the wilderness to be tempted of the devil. And when he had fasted forty days and forty nights...Matthew 4:1-2Remember that the olive trees can stand for long periods of drought, and the olives must be pressed under weight to obtain the oil.Forty has a spiritual meaning - Probation and trial.

The oil from the olives speaks of probation by trial. After Jesus had His time of probation by trial in the wilderness, He came out victorious and started His miraculous ministry.

To remind you, I told you earlier that there is a price to pay to carry a high level of anointing. You will lose your reputation by those you consider as friends, and you can be abandoned by everyone around you.

It will seem as if you are living in the wilderness, but you will be able (by God's grace) to stand long periods of drought. Not many have passed the test of the wilderness.For many are called, but few are chosen.Matthew 22:14

.The anointing is a sign of God's approval over God's chosen vessels. It is not for public demonstration to make a show, but to serve the King of kings.

After one's probation by trial, he will be fit to be a carrier of God's power in a greater level.The word trying or testing in Greek is dokimos.

It means approval. It is a word found on the undersides of many ancient pieces of pottery. This mark dokimosmeans that the piece has gone through the furnace without cracking and has been approved for service.

God's chosen vessels who have been approved for royal service are marked "dokimos."

They don't need the approval of man, and they are always disapproved by those who are governed by the flesh....and blend them into sacred anointed oil.Exodus 30:25 (NABV)According to the instructions of God to Moses after the principal spices had been prepared, they would be blended with olive oil.

The essential element for the blending process.By the help of my best friend, the Holy Spirit, I have given what I believe are the spiritual applications of the spices in an individuals life.

After these characteristics have been formed in one's life through submission and total obedience unto God, then he/she will be found fit to be "blended" by the "apothecary

."And after the blending process, everyone will be able to notice the mark of God's approval upon an individual's life....an ointment compound after the art of the apothecary:...

Exodus 30:25There are some individuals who always try to "make" the anointing through gimmicks, and this does not last. It can be made only by themaster apothecary

- the Holy Spirit!...neither shall ye make any other like it, after the composition of it:Exodus 30:32 (a)The anointing is not to serve fleshly ends. Doing such things is like holding a time bomb or dynamite in one's hands.

If your motive is to make yourself well known, then you have missed the mark....upon man's flesh shall it not be poured.Exodus 30:32 (b)

When the word of God has fullness of authority in our hearts, and we are not following the voice of carnal reason then the dear Master Apothecary is not hindered by fleshly ends....or whosoever putteth any of it upon a stranger, shall even be cut off from his people.

Exodus 30:33One can be in the church and still be unsaved, just as a man in a garage is not a car. He will never walk in the anointing.

THE MASTER APOTHECARY

In modern times, an apothecary is a pharmaceutical chemist. One who is skilled in the preparation and dispensing of medicinal drugs. Now, just imagine a pharmacist who is unskilled, and prepares some medicines for an individual. He could possibly cause a death.

Years ago, I was a co-minister in a certain church (having conviction and peace) and left because of some strange teachings there. I had a friend who was still in that church. I told him that I was leaving to do what I believe the Lord told me to do. When he went to see the pastor with his own will to leave also (without my influence),

the pastor told him that if he would leave "his" church that the anointing over his life will stop flowing. My friend joined me in the ministry and is now my spiritual son and a very anointed man of God.

Had he listened to the unskilled apothecary, he could have been aborted spiritually. But because he listened to the master apothecary, to-this-day he is a carrier of God's anointing. My conclusion over this matter is that the anointing over one's life is in direct relation to the Holy Spirit Himself.

My advice is beware of unskilled apothecaries, aborter of the carriers of God's anointing. They will be judged one day for the sin of spiritual murder, "thou shall not kill."...and the communion of the Holy Ghost, be with you all.2 Corinthians 13:14The word communion in Greek is Koinoia meaning partnership, intercourse, fellowship, association and companionship, to share anything in common

.It gives you an idea of the relationship which a husband and wife have in common being one.The communion of the Holy Spirit speaks of oneness. For so long, many have called the Holy Spirit all sorts of names.

No sir, the Holy Spirit is not an "it," an influence, or the speaking in tongues. He is the Third Person of the Godhead. We must relate to Him as a person and not just an ordinary person, but Divine.The highest price to pay to walk in God's anointing is to know the Holy Spirit

. If you want to know about me, then ask my wife, and you will know everything For fifteen years being in common through our partnership, intercourse, fellowship, association and sharing anything in common, my wife knows everything about me. She will not leave me for all the gold on planet earth.

Therefore, if one knows the Holy Spirit, he will not exchange that relationship for anything else in life. The more I am knowing the Holy Spirit, the more His life is being manifested through me.

My wife and I share the same bed, the same room, same food and the same vision. In spite of our differences, through our relationship, we have become one. She is making every effort not to displease me.

It must be the same with the Holy Spirit."Dear Holy Spirit, can I watch this T.V. program with you or not? Can we buy this article or not? Can we go to that place together? Please, Holy Spirit, if there is anything that will grieve you, help me not to do it."That means common. We must develop this kind of relationship with the Holy Spirit through fellowship.

The foundation of oneness is love. As long as there is love in a marriage, the oneness will not be broken. In 1 Corinthians chapter 13 verse 4 through verse 7, the Bible mentions the characteristics of love.If you violate these characteristics, you will break the oneness.

The Greek physician prescribes a dose of 1 Corinthians 13:4-7 in order not to break the oneness - morning and evening, every day. This potion has been prepared by the Master Apothecary.I admonish you my precious friends to develop a right relationship with the Holy Spirit. Everyday you will have an infusion of His power, and you will never be the same again. Yield yourself totally to Him.

Tell Him about your weakness. Tell Him that without Him you are nothing. Ask Him for forgiveness when you have grieved Him. Worship Him as you worship the Father and the Lord Jesus.

One who walks carnally in the flesh and affection cannot develop a good relationship with the Holy Spirit. If man cannot develop a good relationship with his wife and commits adultery, it will take time to redevelop a good relationship again. You see, there is a price to pay. Many people do much work but have not time to fellowship with God. Fellowship with God must be first, then works will follow. Works which will bear fruits for God's glory.

LEVELS OF THE ANOINTING

But the anointing which you have received from Him abides in you...I John 2:27,According to the word of God, every born-again, Spirit-filled child if God has the anointing in His life. But I believe that every child of God is responsible for keeping and increasing the level of anointing.

That is why some walk in a greater anointing than others within himself.And when the man went out to the east with the line in his hand, he measured one thousand cubits, and he brought me through the waters, the water came up to my ankles.Again he measured one thousand and brought me through the waters, the water came up to my knees. Again he measured one thousand and brought me through, the water came up to my waist.

Again he measured one thousand and it was a river that I could not cross for the water was too deep, water in which one must swim, a river that could not be crossed.Ezekiel 47:3-5.I believe that there are level or degrees of the anointing.

Some walk at the ankle level. Some at the knee level. Some at the waist level, and some swim in the deep. This is due to the degree they dwell in the presence of Almighty God. They are carrying high levels of El-Shaddai's power.I also believe that because of the authority entrusted to God's called apostles and prophets, they are the ones who walk in a stronger anointing. They are always a threat to the kingdom of darkness.

Every church or ministry who relates to the apostolic and prophetic ministries will also carry a strong anointing.In these last days God is restoring and sending His called apostles and prophets to restore the right pattern of His church so that He may release the highest level o

His anointing that any other generation has ever received.We can see that in the book of Ephesians, chapter 4, God says that the five-fold ministry will equip the saints. The word equip from the Greek word katartismosmeans making fully qualified for service.The church must come to the unity of the faith and of the knowledge of the son of God, to a perfect man, to the measure of the stature of the fulness of Christ. The word unity means oneness. It means having a common goal of doing God/s will on planet earth.

UNITY AND THE ANOINTING

And the Lord said, Behold the people is one... and now nothing will be restrained from then, which they have imagined to do.Genesis 11:6.Here we have an image of unity among the people to build a tower. The Lord scattered the people to break the unity among them and stop their evil project.

There is great power issuing from unity. This is why God wants His children to walk in unity. Satan is activating his Machiavellian plan to bring strife and division among God's people. He is trying to stop the flow of that power of which he is so afraid of.I pray for them: I pray not for the world. That they may be one, as those, Father, art in me, and I in Thee, that they also may be one in us: that the world may believe that Thou hast sent me.

And the glory which thou gavest me I have given Thee, that they may be one, even as we are one.John 17:19, 21-22.The prayer Jesus made to the Father for His church two thousand years ago has transcended time and is reaching us today. Walls of divisions are being crumbled. In my own country I am seeing it happen. The spirit of unity is prevalent, and God is moving mightily. Those who open their heart to what God is doing concerning unity will be vessel through which He will spark the fire of the greatest move of His Spirit.

I believe the day is coming when people from big ministries will come to small countries like Mauritius to see with their own eyes that God does not work according to man's greatness.there ariseth a little cloud out of the sea, like a man's hand. And it came to pass in the meanwhile that heavens was black with clouds and wind, and there was a great rain.

1 Kings 18:44-45.Can you see, precious friends what's going on? God has chosen the foolish, the base things and the things that are despised to shame the wise and mighty that no flesh should glory in His presence. A great rain is about to fall. We have to destroy our fleshly made "umbrellas."

What we are seeing is nothing to compare to what is coming.Jesus said in John 17:22, "and the glory which thou gavest me I have given them, that they may be one, even as we are one."If you study in Exodus 25, you will have insight on how God gave instructions to Moses to build the tabernacle according to His pattern. And in chapter 40 of Exodus, after the tabernacle had been set up according to God's pattern

, He manifested His glory in the form of a cloud. The Hebrew word for glory is Shekinah - the visible manifested presence of God.The psalmist said in Psalms 26:8, "I have loved the place where you glory dwelleth."And now, O Father, glorify me together with yourself, with the glory which I had with you before the world was.John 17:5.When Jesus became incarnate,

He "emptied" Himself of the glory that He had with the Father before the foundation of the world - the glory of being equal with God. On earth, Jesus did not use His glory of being equal with God. He was walking in the glory of being baptized in the Holy Spirit. And He has given that glory to the Church for the purpose of unity

.In His earthly walk, Jesus manifested the glory of being the express image of the Father in human form.And through the cross, He would give that glory to the church - through unity. The Church will walk in a high level of God's power.Now remember well that God manifested His glory after Moses had built the tabernacle according to the pattern that was given to him. In Ephesians, chapter 4 and verse 11,

we see the pattern which Jesus gave the church, but instead men have put their hands to building according to the pattern of flesh. The glory of God can bring back the unity of the Spirit.Behold how delightful and how sweet it is for brethren to dwell together in unity (spirit version)It is like the precious oil upon the head, running down upon the beard, upon the beard of Aaron, running down on the collar of his robes. (rsv)Harmony is as refreshing as the dew on Mount Hermon, on the mountain of Israel.

144

(Taylor version)There the Lord bestows His blessing life for evermore. (nebv)

ANOINTED WITH JOY

Psalms 133:1-3,Rejoice in the Lord always: again I say, Rejoice.Philippians 4:4.If you study the letter of Paul to the Philippians, you will notice the circumstances Paul was in when he wrote this letter, and honestly ask yourself, how can Paul in such a situation talk about the joy of the Lord sixteen times?Paul wrote his letter to the Philippians during his first Roman imprisonment.

This church had a great missionary zeal and was consistent in supporting Paul's apostolic ministry. The dominant aspect of this letter is that of triumphant joy.One of the Hebrew words for joy is simachah - meaning carefree, triumphant joy. This is what Paul was talking about when encouraging his brothers and sister on how to be triumphantly joyful in whatever circumstances, and at all time.I have learned from one of my precious friends about the imprisonment of Paul in Rome.

It was not like our modern prison with good food and physical exercise on a sunny day. It was a hole in the earth with no windows, without light and totally black with a horrible smell.It was the central holding tank of the strength of Rome where all toilet water flowed through. Most prisoners died from the smell. Paul was held alive in chains and isolated in complete darkness in a sewage hole.

From time to time, a Roman soldier would come down with a candle and hand over to Paul a writing pen and paper permitting him to write a letter. His only right being that he was a Roman citizen. It was right in that hole that Paul wrote to the Philippians and told them to rejoice in the Lord always. How could Paul rejoice in such a place? It was that joy of the Lord which was sustaining Paul alive.

For I know that this shall turn to my salvation through your prayer, and the supply of the Spirit of Jesus Christ.Philippians 1:19,The Philippians were genuinely upholding Paul in prayer more so than any other church, and the Holy Spirit was supplying supernatural strength to him making him joyful.

The joy of the Lord was being infused in his inner being.Paul had communion with the Holy Spirit. There was oneness between the great duo - the Holy Spirit and Paul.One of the Greek words for joy in the New Testament is Charis - derived from charuo meaning grace. Joy is a direct result of God's grace upon an individual.And he said unto me,

My grace is sufficient for thee, for my strength is made perfect in weakness.2 Corinthians 12:9Charis is the divine influence upon the heart, and its reflection in life. Paul was reflecting that divine power - joy! This kind of joy cannot be affected by any circumstance, but it affects circumstance.My brethren, count it all joy when ye fall into divers temptation;

James 1:2The word "count" in Greek is Hegeoma - meaning to lead, to be the chief, to preside, to govern or rule. Here the writer was saying, "let the JOY that has been infused in you inner man be your leader. Let it preside, govern, and rule over you."

Whatever circumstances you might be facing, it is for the trial of your faith which brings forth patience.The Greek word for patience is Hupomonc - meaning the capacity to abide and resist under pressure.

God wants to produce in His beloved children the divine capacity to resist whatever pressure of life and walk out triumphant with joy - making us perfect after the patience process. The word perfect in Greek is Teleios meaning full grown, fully developed adult.... The oil of joy for mourning, the garment of praise for the spirit of heaviness, that they may be called trees of righteousness, the planting of the Lord, that He may be glorified. Isaiah 61:3

THE ENEMY OF THE ANOINTING

We have learned during our study that our relationship with the Master Apothecary must be a perfect one through oneness because the anointing upon our lives depends on that relationship. Like a husband and wife, there is only one thing that can break the oneness between them and that's adultery. So the oneness between the Holy Spirit and a child of God in the same way can be broken. and it should not have to be so.Satan will try by any means to break this oneness through any open door in order to stop the flow of the anointing in our lives.

As far as I can understand by the Holy Spirit, I want to help my beloved brothers and sisters to know what can stop the flow of God's anointing in our lives.And grieve not the Holy Spirit of God, whereby ye are sealed unto the day of redemption.Ephesians 4:30.Yet they rebelled and grieved His Holy Spirit; only then was he changed into their enemy...Isaiah 63:10 (NEBV)

In grieving the Holy Spirit, you make the Holy Spirit your enemy. When one gives his/her body in intimate relations to another person other than his/her legal partner, it causes grief, sorrow or sadness an separation.How can one grieve the Holy Spirit

?Neither give place to the devil.Ephesians 4:27.The Greek word for place is Topos where we derive such words as Topography. It is used for a region, a locality, area or place which is occupied by a thing or person(s). Therefore, giving a place to the devil for occupying rather than to the Holy Spirit, we break our intimacy with Him. This is committing spiritual adultery.

How does someone give place or access to the devil?If men comply with their lower nature, their thoughts are shaped by the lower nature.Romans 8:5 (Weymouth version)...but those who follow after the Holy Spirit find themselves doing these things that please God.Romans 8:5 (Taylor version)

The mind which is interested only in carnal things is enmity to God.Romans 8:7 (Norlie version).In the book of Romans, Galatians and Ephesians, etc., you have a long list of how many Christians nourish and affectionate their carnal nature and walk. There is also a long list of how we as Christians are advised to affectionate our mind with spiritual things.

Idleness is causing Christians to abstain from Bible study and meditation on the word of God. Sometimes when you see Christians of five to ten years in the church as pew-warmers, it brings shame for the way they are living.Often some questions may arise like, "Hey, how can such and so live in sin and walk in the power of God."How are the mighty fallen in the midst of the battle.

2 Samuel 1:25The shield of Saul, as though he had not been anointed with oil.2 Samuel 1:21Sad to say, the day when mighty soldiers of God fall into sin always comes, it they don't repent.Do you remember Samson of old?

There was a time in Israel when the Philistines were giving a hard time to the people of God because of the evil done by them in the sight of the Lord their God. In His mercy, God sent a deliverer in the person of Samson.

There wasn't a man or army strong enough to stand against Samson as long as he carried God's anointing upon his life. He was giving a hard time to the enemy, and the roles reversed.But satan was watching and looking for a place in the life of Samson to occupy, and he found a place.

The instrument of defeat was used in the hand of the enemy, Delilah. Finally, Samson took the bait and was hooked. In losing his seven locks of hair on his head (a symbol of his consecration unto God), Samson lost his anointing. He was defeated. Character building goes hand in hand with the anointing. You build your character in the school of the Holy Spirit, not human made in a school. Character makes you stand, and the anointing is for effective service. Many precious servants of God have the anointing,

but not Godly character. You must have both.Delilah comes from a root Hebrew word day - meaning to be feeble, be emptied, to fail, to dry up or to languish. To languish means to lose strength, to become weak. Delilah is watching for an open door in our lives in order to languish the anointing. So when we try to fight back, we will not be able to make it and be defeated.

Church, this is not the time to play. It is the time to rise up in the power of God, shouting the battle-cry, and together joining our hands and enforcing Calvary's victory.Arise from the depression and prostration in which circumstances have kept you: rise to a new life! Shine - be radiant with the glory of the Lord! For the light is come and the glory of the Lord is risen upon you!Isaiah 60:1 (Amplified version)

THE BLESSINGS OF
THE FRESH OIL ANOINTING

I am anointed with fresh oil.Psalms 92:10 (ABPS version)I have noticed that there are many sincere ministers (I was one of them) who dwell on what God did yesterday. They try to make things work on the anointing which was on them yesterday. It is here where satan, the counterfeiter, is seducing many of our precious ones.God does not make duplication but originals.

When in service, oil always loses its thickness and in due time must be replaced by fresh oil. Just like the oil in the engine of your vehicle can cause damage if it's not changed every 3000 miles. We, as serving the Lord, need a daily infusion of God's fresh anointing.

There is no substitution for any child of God to dwell in the presence of El Shaddai daily in communion and not come out with a fresh anointing.Who shall ascend into the hill of the Lord? Or who shall stand in His holy place? He that hath clean hands a pure heart; who hath not lifted up his soul unto vanity, nor sworn righteousness from the God of his salvation. This is the generation of them that seek Him that seek Thy face, O Jacob.Psalms 24:3-6Daily communion with the Father, Son and Holy Ghost must be our priority. It must not fit according to our time table

. We always have time for everything in life, but not time for fellowship with God.We have time to preach, that's good.Time to read Christian books, that's good.But what about our priority? This is what our God is longing for, His children to dwell daily in His presence.Through Psalm 92 verses 10 to 15, we will study about the blessings of the fresh anointing.Promotion,But my horn shall thou exalt like the horn of an unicorn: I shall be anointed with fresh oil.Palms 92:10

But you have promoted me, so that I am like a powerful buffalo; I am anointed with fresh oil.Psalms 92:10 (Harrison version)The first blessing of walking in the fresh anointing is promotion. I personally never met anyone who does not like to be promoted. The Bible says in Psalms 75 that promotion comes neither from the east nor from the south, but from God.

The word horn is from the Hebrew word Geren which is symbolic of strength, power and victory. The word promotion is from the Hebrew word Fumm meaningto rise or raise, to bring up or to exalt. This is what God wants to do with His children.Perception,Mine eyes also shall see my desire on mine enemies

.Psalms 92:11The word perceive means to have insight, to discern, to see, to consider, to give ear, to understand and to hear intelligently....and anoint your eyes with eye salve, that you may see.Revelation 3:18...and do not know that you are blind Revelation 3:17The church of Laodicea had become self satisfied. They were blinded and self-satisfied with material wealth. They said that they now needed nothing.

They became lukewarm without the fresh anointing.Jesus said to Laodicea to anoint their eyes with eye salve. Laodicea had the reputation of producing salve for the curing of eye disorders. Having become spiritually blind, Jesus told them that they needed the fresh anointing added to their spiritual blindness in order to regain good perception. Like many churches who are dead today needing the fresh anointing to cure their spiritual blindness. Walking in the fresh anointing will allow the children of God to have insight on what is going on and discern between the genuine and the counterfeit.

SENSITIVITY

Without being spiritually sensitive, we will not be able to hear the voice of God. Dwelling and listening in the presence of God will develop our spiritual sensitivity.If ever I call for my wife or one of my two children, whomever I call for will answer and come to me. Why?

By being in the same house and living together for years, we know each other's voice. Our natural sensitivity has been developed. It is the same thing with God.Then He openeth the ears of men. (KJV)
Then He makes His secrets clear to men. (Basic English version)
Then it is He whispers in the ears of man. (Jerusalem version)
HE SPEAKS WORDS OF REVELATION.

Job 33:16Many are not hearing what the Holy Spirit is saying. Those who walk in the fresh anointing have good spiritual sensitivity and can hear the voice of God

.Productivity.The righteous shall flourish like the palm tree; he shall grow like a cedar in Lebanon. Those that be planted in the house of the Lord shall flourish in the courts of our God. They shall still bring forth fruit in old age; they shall be fat and flourishing. Psalms 92:12-

.Another blessing of the fresh anointing is that you will become fertile and able to produce., Too many children of God are not reaching their potential to produce for God's glory, and they remain sterile.In John, the fifteenth chapter, Jesus says, those who do not produce fruit are cut away by His Father, and He purges those who bear fruit. I conclude that our Father does not tolerate non-productivity because He has provided everything needed for His children to be productive.

DECLARATION

Eager to declare that the Lord is just, the Lord my rock, in whom there is no unrighteousness. Psalm 92:15 (NEBV)In chapter two, I wrote about the five ingredients of the anointing oil. Five speaks of grace.

We also have, by God's grace five benefits of the fresh anointing according to Psalm 92 verses 10 through 15 in our study.There are too many "mouth-closed: Christians nowadays. They are afraid to open their mouths to speak about Jesus, but when they gossip, then their mouths are "wide-opened" by a counterfeit "anointing."

This is why the harvest is being delayed. When one is anointed with fresh oil, he will not be able to close his mouth. He will speak about the grace of the Almighty God....and my mouth was opened, and

I was no more dumb.Ezekiel 33:22Many Christians need deliverance from spiritual dumbness. They need the fresh anointing for them to declare the goodness of God.Now numerous Samaritans from that town believed on and trusted in Him because of what the woman said when she declared and testified.John 4:39 Amplified version).

To declare means to make known, to announce openly. Too many ministers are busy making themselves well known and are making Jesus unknown. We, as God's servants, must not become celebrities, but we must celebrate Jesus. If not, the Lord will stop the flow of His anointing on our lives and all resources will bankrupt.

And if you and we belong to Christ guaranteed as His and anointed, it is all God's doing.
2 Corinthians 1:21 (NEBV)

WHAT CAUSES THE ANOINTING

What causes the Power or Anointing to be present, or enabled to be tapped into?Since the death, burial, and resurrection of Jesus we have had available to us the Anointing or Power of God. The healing power of God is made available to them that become aware of it.

When the Word of God is being spoken or read to us, by ourselves or someone else, then the power of God is available to save, heal, deliver, etc. When we read the scriptures on healing the power to be healed is contained in those scriptures and made available to us through His Spirit. Hebrews 4:12, "

The word of God is quick and powerful, and sharper than any two edged sword."Faith comes as a result of the spoken word, thus enabling the power of God to accommodate those who believe:- Romans 10: 9-14, "We believe and spoke resulting in our salvation". - 2nd Peter 1:3, "His devine power has granted to us everything pertaining to life and godliness." - Romans 10:17, "Faith comes by hearing the word of God

."Our obedience to the word of God brings the power within the word of God to meet our healing or deliverance. No obedience, no power! Romans 6:17-18, "But God be thanked, that ye were the servants of sin, but ye have obeyed from the heart that form of doctrine which was delivered you. Being then made free from sin, ye became the servants of righteousness."In Mark 4 we see a powerful example of the seed or word of God that Jesus describes in the parable of the sower

. A natural seed will produce fruit, and He said that the word of God planted on good soil would produce some 30,60, and 100 fold.In Luke 5:17 we see that Jesus was teaching, "and the power of the Lord was present to heal." The power becomes present when there is teaching on the Word of God, for healing, salvation, deliverance, etc.

The anointing also comes at times as the direct Will of God through manifestations of the Holy Spirit in and through our lives or others in the body of Christ. We can call this special anointing as the Spirit wills (1st cor. 12:7-11). Anytime you have a manifestation Of one or more of the gifts of the Holy Spirit in operation,

the power to perform that gift is in operation.We see this in the ministry of Jesus as He ministered in two main methods. First through teaching and preaching the word of God and secondly through allowing the Holy Spirit to use Him as the Father willed and directed through the Holy Spirit

. An example in John 5:1-13 is the impotent man that was by the Sheep Gate in Bethesda. The man did not know about Jesus. He did not have faith of his own. It was through Jesus, directed to him by the Spirit of God as a soveriegn will and expression of the Father, that the man through the ministry of Jesus was healed.

THE OIL WILL NOT RUN DRY IF YOU'RE OPEN TO RECEIVE A NEW ANOINTING. ASK GOD FOR IT, THEN ASK HIM FOR JARS INTO WHICH THE OIL CAN BE POURED.

If I had to choose one distinctive element of our ministry, it would be that we have been channels of restoration and spiritual renewal for both individuals and ministries. Hundreds of thousands of people who have attended our meetings around the world have testified to a fresh anointing that brought lasting changes to their lives, their communion with God and their Christian service.

But wherever I go I hear the same question: "Pastor Claudio, what do I do to keep the anointing flowing?"All over the world, believers express similar concerns about keeping their anointing fresh. Some who are filled with oil and burning with the fire of the Holy Spirit are afraid of losing that wonderful communion with God. Others, whose jars have broken, have lost oil along the way. For them the question becomes a particularly urgent one.

LESSONS FROM A PROPHET

I believe Elijah has something to teach us about keeping the anointing flowing. Consider his encounter with the widow at Zarephath. He comes upon her as she prepares a fire for the last meal she and her son expect to have.When Elijah asks for bread and water, she tells him they have run out of food; all they have left is a handful of flour and a little oil. When that is gone, she and her son will die.This situation illustrates the condition of many believers.

They are God's children, and the oil of the Holy Spirit is in their lives. But their spiritual lives are as good as dead--they barely have any oil in their jugs.There is very little anointing. They have a devotional life, but it

159

is carried out with great effort, almost as a burden. They serve the Lord, but without any fruit.Many Christians, aware that their situation is like that of the widow of Zarephath, prepare themselves for their spiritual death.

They resign themselves to living Christian lives without joy, power or sparkle. They live their faith without expectation, just waiting to die.But Elijah gave the widow a list of instructions to prevent the oil from running out. Let's examine these instructions together.Examine your attitude. The first order Elijah gave the widow had to do with maintaining a correct attitude. "Don't be afraid," he told her (1 Kings 17:13). The widow at Zarephath had to stop believing that she and her son were going to die. She had to free her mind of negative thoughts and unbelief

.Unfortunately, a spirit of fear holds many Christians in bondage and hinders them from living an abundant life. The moment some Christians have a new experience with the Lord, they start thinking, I wonder how long this will last.Maybe they have allowed the flame of God's fire to go out and now feel unqualified to start all over again. Or perhaps they are afraid of losing the fresh anointing they have received. We cannot permit ourselves to become immersed in unbelief, doubts and fear.When God anointed you with His Holy Spirit, He didn't give you a spirit of timidity or fear. The oil that descended upon you is the spirit of love, power and self-control (see 2 Tim. 1:7).

Don't believe the lie that your Christian life will die a slow death, that your fellowship with God is fading. Don't accept as normal a substandard life when it comes to witnessing and service. Don't be paralyzed by fear so you end up losing all God has given you. If you follow the instructions in the Word, the oil of the anointing of the Holy Spirit will not run dry.Establish your priorities. Elijah's second recommendation addresses priorities

. When the woman told him her problem, Elijah had an interesting response: "Go home and do as you have said. But first make a small cake of bread for me from what you have and bring it to me, and then make something for yourself and your son" (1 Kings 17:13).The word first is significant. Elijah appears to be insensitive. Although he knew that this poor widow had little food, he asked her to provide food for him first. But in doing so Elijah was applying a basic principle for receiving God's blessing

.This principle applies to our finances, but it also applies to everything else. Do you want blessings in your family life, your studies, your vocation, your profession, your relationships and your ministry? Then apply the priorities principle.Give first to God; God, who doesn't owe anybody anything, will give you what you need and even more. Consecrate your life to God. Let Him be the most important thing in your life

.I have ministered to thousands and thousands of people, and I have never known anyone who, having put Jesus first in his or her life, has ever lost the intensity of the anointing.

Be obedient. The third precept is that of obedience.Try to place yourself in the widow's situation. You are in the midst of a catastrophic national crisis. Because of a drought, there is no food.All you have left is a handful of flour and a little oil in a jug. All you can do is eat and then dieBut suddenly, someone appears and tells you, "Before you and your son eat, give me something's

." What would you have done? What would you have said?When the Potter places His hands on you and molds you as His jar, He fills you with oil so you can be a blessing to others. Disobedience ruins the jar and causes the oil to spill.Many believers are anointed by God to minister with signs and wonders. God commands them to pray for the sick in His name so He may heal them.But instead of following God's instructions, they become afraid, lose their faith and end up disobeying. They do this over and over again until God cannot trust them any longer.

And so, very slowly, the anointing decreases.God touches other believers, fills them with joy, gives them external evidences so they learn to trust and fills them to overflowing with His love. They receive the anointing but continue with sin in their lives.They want the anointing of power, but they are not willing to abandon those things that grieve Him who gives the anointing. Anointing and sin can't walk together too far. Either the anointing gets rid of the sin or the sin gets rid of the anointing because darkness has no fellowship with light.

TIME WITH GOD Elijah told the widow to go home. God was going to do an amazing thing in her life, and she needed to be at home.The believer has to understand the importance of time alone with God. In recent years we have seen church services filled with people who praise God together and want to be ministered to. This is wonderful, but we cannot neglect our private time with God.

Our anointing for public ministry corresponds directly to the time we spend alone with God.There is no secret formula in this. Anointed men and women who have been raised up by God in each generation have been those whose prayer lives were rich and consistent.Prayer must be a daily practice for every believer. We must be alone with Him as much as possible--not only to seek more of Him but also to see our anointing increase. Jesus practiced this in His own life, pulling away to be alone with His Father. There, He received more holy anointing.

SHARING THE ANOINTING Elijah and Elisha not only had similar names, they also had similar ministries. In 2 Kings we read that Elisha also performed a miracle of provision for a widow. In this case, it was a prophet's widow. Her husband had revered God, but he had died, and there were debts to pay.Since she didn't have the means to pay, the creditor wanted to take her two sons as his slaves.

When Elisha asked what she had in her house, she answered, "Your servant has nothing there at all... except a little oil" (2 Kings 4:2).Elisha told the widow what to do with the jar of oil--but his instructions sounded strange and a bit ridiculous: "Go around and ask all your neighbors for empty jars. Don't ask for just a few.

Then go inside and shut the door behind you and your sons. Pour oil into all the jars, and as each is filled, put it to one side" (vv. 3-4).

Asking the neighbors for oil instead of jars would have made a bit more sense to me. The oil was valuable and negotiable and therefore could have provided money to pay the creditor, whereas the jars had very little value.But Elisha ordered her to ask for jars!For the anointing not to run dry, we have to share it. So many believers spend their time praying for more anointing, more oil. But God is telling them, "Don't ask for oil; ask for more jars. If there are more jars, I will pour more oil, and the oil of My anointing will never cease

."The Word says that the widow's jars became filled with oil. The sons kept bringing more jars, and instead of running dry, the oil kept on flowing, filling more and more jars. It ceased to flow when there were no more jars to fill.The oil of the anointing will cease when you stop finding jars with which to share your blessings. As long as there are new jars to hold the Holy Spirit's oil, the anointing will go on.

VESSELS TO FILL

The people around you--at home, at work, in the neighborhood, in your school--are empty jars. They are needy, lacking all those things that only Jesus Christ can produce in people's lives.

When you bless them, two things happen. They are filled, and your oil continues to flow even more.Remember too that blessing those around you is only the beginning. God expects that, but He also wants your influence to reach to the ends of the world.

The jars the widow needed had three characteristics: They had to be borrowed from the neighbors, they had to be empty and they had to be not "just a few" (v. 3). If you ask for jars and not just oil, God will send you people to minister to and bless.All of a sudden you will start seeing people in a new way; the Holy Spirit will show you needs that lie deep in their hearts.

You will be able to minister to them in a specific way, and the anointing will go with you and increase in you. The only time the oil runs dry is when there are no more vessels to fill.The Potter formed you and made you into a jar

. When you are filled with the oil of the Spirit, you bless those around you. If you are feeling as hopeless as the widow of Zarephath, do not allow your spiritual life to die but be open to receive a new anointing.If you have asked for oil, you have received God's anointing already. Now ask for jars, and share the oil with them.

PRAYER DOES NOT INCREASE YOUR ANOINTING!

Yet let me clarify, prayer does not increase your anointing. Nope it does not! (Against popular beliefs). Prayer is not a ignition to get the anointing going. Prayer is what increases the intimacy in your relationship with God. And no, neither does it make God love you anymore than how much He loved you on the cross, but prayer helps you to tune into that reality of love

.Prayer cuts you from the noise of the world and tunes you to the voice of the Holy Spirit. In this process of being connected to the vine, the anointing/power of God flows in through us (the branches).

Anointing therefore is only a by product of prayer. Some seem to think that more anointed is to do more impressive things. Simply not how God views it

. A simple example to explain this is, if God has anointed a person to reach villages for Jesus, that man praying for months is not going to change him into a mega church preacher. His anointing to fulfill his call and purpose does not change with prayer. Prayer only tunes him to fulfill His primary purpose.

THEN HOW DOES THE ANOINTING INCREASE?

Anointing has been described to work in stages. What I believe is that when a person is anointed by God for the working of miracles, his increase in prayer life does not increase that anointing

, but what increases with prayer is his sensitivity to understand God direction, guidance or will for the different situations that he faces.

Reading dozens of the chapters of the Bible is not what makes you more anointed, but it increases one's faith to believe God to function in the anointing God has placed on one's life.It has always interested me that God called His disciples Apostles even before they planted any church. What is more interesting is that the Judas that betrayed him was also in the company of those that were called as Apostles. Anointing is God's calling on one's life. Not something that can be bought. How we respond to that call is on us. That means, your anointing is activated from the call you have received and multiplies according to your levels of faith.Explaining that in <u>Romans 12: 6</u>.

"We have different gifts, according to the grace given to us. If a man's gift is prophesying, let him use it in proportion to his faith." (NIV).So in the first place it clarifies what I said earlier in my previous post– there is nothing you can do to deserve God's anointing.

We have <u>gifts that empower</u> the body of Christ according to the grace given to us. And notice the second part how a man's gift is proportionate to the faith in God.Your <u>faith</u> increases by hearing the Word of God, the more you immerse yourself in prayer and faith

, the more you are tuned to Him. And the anointing in your life is further activated(to do what you were purposed for) with that faith that is birthed out of the intimacy with God.Thereby anointing is contagious because faith is contagious. Anointing can be rubbed off, because faith of one man stirs another. So now, go immerse yourself in God and put your faith into action!

HOW TO KNOW THE ANOINTING OF GOD

1.   WHAT IS GOD'S ANOINTING?

It is knowing the supernatural presence of God upon us, being aware of His presence with us. A physical experience where we feel the warm presence and glow of God upon our body.

2.   JESUS CHRIST KNEW THE ANOINTING OF GOD

Acts 10:38: "how God anointed Jesus of Nazareth with the Holy Spirit and with power, who went about doing good and healing all who were oppressed by the devil, for God was with Him."

3.   THE SECRET OF THE ANOINTING

John 8:29: "And He who sent Me is with Me. The Father has not left Me alone, for I always do those things that please Him."

Obedience is necessary: John 8:47: "He who is of God hears God's words; therefore you do not hear, because you are not of God."

4.   WITH THE ANOINTING COMES GOD'S HEALING

Healing of the woman with the fountain of blood.Mark 5:27-34: "When she heard about Jesus, she came behind Him in the crowd and touched

His garment. For she said, "If only I may touch His clothes, I shall be made well." Immediately the fountain of her blood was dried up, and she felt in her body that she was healed of the affliction. And Jesus, immediately knowing in Himself that power had gone out of Him, turned around in the crowd and said, "Who touched My clothes?" But His disciples said to Him, "You see the multitude thronging You, and You say, Who touched Me?'" And He looked around to see her who had done this thing. But the woman, fearing and trembling, knowing what had happened to her, came and fell down before Him and told Him the whole truth. And He said to her, 'Daughter, your faith has made you well. Go in peace, and be healed of your affliction."

5. POWERFUL ANOINTING ON JESUS - RAISING FROM THE DEAD.

Mark 5:41-42: "Then He took the child by the hand, and said to her, 'Talitha, cumi,'which is translated, 'Little girl, I say to you, arise." Immediately the girl arose and walked, for she was twelve years of age. And they were overcome with great amazement."

6. WHEN DID THE ANOINTING COME UPON JESUS?

Matthew 3:16-17: "When He had been baptized, Jesus came up immediately from the water; and behold, the heavens were opened to Him, and He saw the Spirit of God descending like a dove and alighting upon Him. And suddenly a voice came from heaven, saying, "This is My beloved Son, in whom I am well pleased."

He began to preach: Matthew 4:17: "From that time Jesus began to preach and to say, "Repent, for the kingdom of heaven is at hand."

He was able to say (Luke 4:18-19): "The Spirit of the LORD is upon Me, Because He has anointed Me To preach the gospel to the poor; He has sent Me to heal the brokenhearted, To proclaim liberty to the captives

And recovery of sight to the blind, To set at liberty those who are oppressed; To proclaim the acceptable year of the LORD."
He had authority: Luke 4:32: "And they were astonished at His teaching, for His word was with authority."

Demons began to cry out: Luke 4:34: "saying, "Let us alone! What have we to do with You, Jesus of Nazareth? Did You come to destroy us? I know who You are - the Holy One of God!"Many were healed: Luke 4:40: "When the sun was setting, all those who had any that were sick with various diseases brought them to Him; and He laid His hands on every one of them and healed them."
Demons came out of many: Luke 4:41: "And demons also came out of many, crying out and saying, "You are the Christ, the Son of God!" And He, rebuking them, did not allow them to speak, for they knew that He was the Christ."

7.   CAN THIS ANOINTING BE QUENCHED?

Yes, by unbelief. Mark 6:5: "Now He could do no mighty work there, except that He laid His hands on a few sick people and healed them."

8.   SHOULD WE EXPECT TO KNOW THAT SAME ANOINTING?

Yes. 1 John 2:20: "But you have an anointing from the Holy One, and you know all things."Note:We have an anointing. This is further confirmed in:1 John 2:27: "But the anointing which you have received from Him abides in you, and you do not need that anyone teach you; but as the same anointing teaches you concerning all things, and is true, and is not a lie, and just as it has taught you, you will abide in Him."

RESULT OF KNOWING ANOINTING

The operation of the gifts of the Spirit.

Word of wisdom   Gift of prophecy

Word of knowledge   Discerning of spirits

Gift of faith   Kinds of tongues

Gift of healing   Interpretation of tongues

Working of miracles

9.   HOW DO WE COME TO KNOW THIS ANOINTING?

Scriptural background: Exodus 30:22-30: "Moreover the LORD spoke to Moses, saying:] "Also take for yourself quality spices - five hundred shekels of liquid myrrh, half as much sweet-smelling cinnamon (two hundred and fifty shekels), two hundred and fifty shekels of sweet-smelling cane, "five hundred shekels of cassia, according to the shekel of the sanctuary, and a hin of olive oil.

"And you shall make from these a holy anointing oil, an ointment compounded according to the art of the perfumer. It shall be a holy anointing oil. "With it you shall anoint the tabernacle of meeting and the ark of the Testimony; "the table and all its utensils, the lampstand and its utensils, and the altar of incense; "the altar of burnt offering with all its utensils, and the laver and its base.

"You shall consecrate them, that they may be most holy; whatever touches them must be holy. "And you shall anoint Aaron and his sons, and consecrate them, that they may minister to Me as priests."

Moses fulfilled these commandments: Leviticus 8:10-12: "Also Moses took the anointing oil, and anointed the tabernacle and all that was in it, and consecrated them. He sprinkled some of it on the altar seven times, anointed the altar and all its utensils, and the laver and its base, to consecrate them.

And he poured some of the anointing oil on Aaron's head and anointed him, to consecrate him."The sons of Aaron were also anointed.Leviticus 8:30: "Then Moses took some of the anointing oil and some of the blood which was on the altar, and sprinkled it on Aaron, on his garments, on his sons, and on the garments of his sons with him; and he consecrated Aaron, his garments, his sons, and the garments of his sons with him."

10.   SETTING APART FOR SERVICE

The anointing of God means being set apart for His service.Samuel anointed Saul. 1 Samuel 10:1: "Then Samuel took a flask of oil and poured it on his head, and kissed him and said: "Is it not because the LORD has anointed you commander over His inheritance?"Samuel anointed David. 1 Samuel 16:13: "Then Samuel took the horn of oil and anointed him in the midst of his brothers; and the Spirit of the LORD came upon David from that day forward. So Samuel arose and went to

."However, a distressing spirit came on Saul.1 Samuel 16:14: "But the Spirit of the LORD departed from Saul, and a distressing spirit from the LORD troubled him."This was because of his disobedience to God.King Solomon. King David instructed that his son, Solomon, be anointed King over Israel. 1 Kings 1:39: "Then Zadok the priest took a horn of oil from the tabernacle and anointed Solomon. And they blew the horn, and all the people said, "Long live King Solomon!"

11.   THE ANOINTING OF JEHU AS KING OF ISRAEL

1 Kings 19:16-17:   "Also you shall anoint Jehu the son of Nimshi as king over Israel. And Elisha the son of Shaphat of Abel Meholah you shall anoint as prophet in your place.   "It shall be that whoever escapes the sword of Hazael, Jehu will kill; and whoever escapes the sword of Jehu, Elisha will kill."The anointing of Jehu in the book of 2 Kings.   2 Kings 9:1-3:   "

And Elisha the prophet called one of the sons of the prophets, and said to him, "Get yourself ready, take this flask of oil in your hand, and go to Ramoth Gilead.   "Now when you arrive at that place, look there for Jehu the son of Jehoshaphat, the son of Nimshi, and go in and make him rise up from among his associates, and take him to an inner room.   "Then take the flask of oil, and pour it on his head, and say, 'Thus says the LORD: "I have anointed you king over Israel."' Then open the door and flee, and do not delay."

12.   JOASH WAS ANOINTED KING OF JUDAH

2 Kings 11:12:   "And he brought out the king's son, put the crown on him, and gave him the Testimony; they made him king and anointed him, and they clapped their hands and said, "Long live the king!"

Jehoahaz, son of Josiah, was anointed King in his place.2 Kings 23:30:   "Then his servants moved his body in a chariot from Megiddo, brought him to Jerusalem, and buried him in his own tomb. And the people of the land took Jehoahaz the son of Josiah, anointed him, and made him king in his father's place."

13.   CONCLUSION:

The Old Testament contains a clear pattern of the anointing of priests, prophets and kings, such anointing being with oil made according to the recipe which God gave to Moses.

Illustration of the anointing: Psalm 133: "Behold, how good and how pleasant it is For brethren to dwell together in unity! It is like the precious oil upon the head, Running down on the beard, The beard of Aaron, Running down on the edge of his garments. It is like the dew of Hermon, Descending upon the mountains of Zion; For there the LORD commanded the blessing - Life forevermore."

14.   WHAT ABOUT THE BELIEVERS?

(a)   We have received an anointing.
   (1 John 2:20; 1 John 2:27)
   2 Corinthians 1:21: "Now He who establishes us with you in Christ and has anointed us is God,"
(b)   How does this happen?
   By being born again. John 3:3: "Jesus answered and said to him, "Most assuredly, I say to you, unless one is born again, he cannot see the kingdom of God."
(c)   We then become Priests and Kings:
1 Peter 2:9: "But you are a chosen generation, a royal priesthood, a holy nation, His own special people, that you may proclaim the praises of Him who called you out of darkness into His marvelous light;"
   Revelation 1:6: "and has made us kings and priests to God and His Father, to Him be glory and dominion forever and ever. Amen."
(d)   **WILL GOD ANOINT US?** Yes, we have received the spirit of adoption. Romans 8:15: "For you did not receive the spirit of bondage again to fear, but you received the Spirit of adoption by whom we cry out, "Abba, Father."

15. THE HOLY SPIRIT IS A PERSON

John 16:7-13   "Nevertheless I tell you the truth. It is to your advantage that I go away; for if I do not go away, the Helper will not come to you; but if I depart, I will send Him to you.   "And when He has come, He will convict the world of sin, and of righteousness, and of judgment: "of sin, because they do not believe in Me;   "of righteousness, because I go to My Father and you see Me no more;   "of judgment, because the ruler of this world is judged.   "I still have many things to say to you, but you cannot bear them now.   "However, when He, the Spirit of truth, has come, He will guide you into all truth; for He will not speak on His own authority, but whatever He hears He will speak; and He will tell you things to come."

16. WE SHOULD BE BAPTISED WITH THE HOLY SPIRIT

Acts 2:1-4:   "When the Day of Pentecost had fully come, they were all with one accord in one place.   And suddenly there came a sound from heaven, as of a rushing mighty wind, and it filled the whole house where they were sitting.   Then there appeared to them divided tongues, as of fire, and one sat upon each of them.   And they were all filled with the Holy Spirit and began to speak with other tongues, as the Spirit gave them utterance."

17. THE ANOINTING IS FOR TODAY

(1 John 2:20&27)

18. HOW DO WE FEEL THIS ANOINTING?

Just as the anointing oil was poured on the head of Aaron and over his beard, so we can feel the anointing oil of the Holy Spirit as it descends upon us.

19. THE ANOINTING BREAKS THE YOKE

Isaiah 10:27: "It shall come to pass in that day That his burden will be taken away from your shoulder, And his yoke from your neck, And the yoke will be destroyed because of the anointing oil."

Breaks yoke of sickness, disease and depression.

20. BLOCKAGES TO THE ANOINTING

(a) Failure to honour parents and forgive them.

(b) Failure to renounce the sins of ancestors.

(c) Failure to renounce wrong doctrine, fear, doubt, unbelief and unforgiveness.

(d) Failure to break with the occult.

21. OCCASIONS OF GOD'S ANOINTING

(a) By the Word of God. We need to be a disciplined reader of the Word of God.

(b) Praise and worship. We should enter into praise and worship regularly.

(c) Salvation. As we really come to know the Lord, the anointing of God enters us.

(d) When there is healing and deliverance from demons great anointing occurs.

(e) Testimony. When one is giving their testimony the anointing will frequently fall on the meeting.

(f) Preaching the Word. When the preacher speaks from his heart and reads the Word of God with belief, the anointing will fall.

(g) Gifts of the Holy Spirit. When the preacher is operating in the word of knowledge, word of wisdom, discernment of spirits and other gifts, the people sense the power of God present.

(h)   Prayer and fasting.   During times of prayer and fasting the anointing of God can be felt.

(i)   Walking in the will of God.   When all our thoughts and actions are centred on God through Jesus Christ and we are seeking to follow His will, we will frequently sense the anointing of God.

(j)   When two or more are gathered in the name of Jesus Christ.   When there is a gathering of persons committed to the Lordship of Jesus Christ or who are seeking such commitment and who begin to put aside all doubt, fear and unbelief, then the anointing of God falls on the gathering.

(k)   Repentance.   When there is a true attitude of repentance and acts of repentance, then the anointing will frequently manifest.

22.   FRAGRANCE OF THE HOLY SPIRIT

This can be present in meetings and is referred to in Psalm 45:6-8: "Your throne, O God, is forever and ever; A sceptre of righteousness is the sceptre of Your kingdom.   You love righteousness and hate wickedness; Therefore God, Your God, has anointed You With the oil of gladness more than Your companions.   All Your garments are scented with myrrh and aloes and cassia, Out of the ivory palaces, by which they have made You glad."

23.   WE NEED THE ANOINTING

We need the anointing of God more than ever today.   As we know that anointing, the yoke is broken and healings, deliverances and mighty miracles can take place.

24.   HOW TO KNOW GOD'S ANOINTING

(a)   Surrender absolutely to the Lordship of Jesus Christ.

(b)   Believe the Word of God in its entirety.

(c)   If you have never received any form of water baptism, ensure that you are baptised in water, thus identifying with Jesus Christ in His death and His resurrection.

(d) Repent from all sin, especially unbelief, doubt, fear, things of the occult, unforgiveness, blockage of mind, wrong doctrine.

(e) Be baptised with the Holy Spirit.

(f) Read again the Scriptures in 1 John 2:20 and 2:27 which confirm that we have an anointing from the Holy One.

(g) Go on your knees and say a simple prayer such as this:

"Dear Heavenly Father, I come to You in the name of Your Son Jesus Christ

. I praise You Lord and I worship You and I thank You that You love me so much that You sent Your Son, Jesus Christ, to die for me and pay the penalty for my sins. I believe that I am reconciled to You through the blood of Jesus Christ and that I have received Your peace. I renounce all sin, everything of the occult, all unbelief, all fear, all doubt, wrong doctrine, blockage of mind. These I renounce in the name of Jesus Christ and I ask You Lord to let me know that anointing which You have already given me by the Holy Spirit. I confess that Jesus Christ is risen from the dead."

(h) If you will do this with all your heart then you will sense the peace of God coming around you and you will feel the physical warmth of the Holy Spirit descending upon your body. You will know for a certainty the anointing of God as a physical presence of God upon your body. As the love of God begins to be shed abroad in your heart by the Holy Spirit, you will feel the physical presence of God around you or on some part of your body.Note: Involvement in the occult blocks the anointing

HOW TO DESTROY THE ANOINTING

1. **WE EXPLOITED IT.** The first attempt at quenching the Spirit's power in the New Testament church was made by Ananias and Sapphira, who were full of greed (see Acts 5:1-11). The same thing happened to the charismatic movement in the 1980s, when prosperity preachers with dollar signs in their eyes showed up to merchandise the Spirit's anointing. Swaggering evangelists in white suits and Rolexes began pushing people to the floor and convincing crowds to dig into their wallets to give in "miracle" offerings. And so began the slow but steady sell-out. We didn't realize the greed was driving us farther and farther from the Spirit's blessing.

2. **WE FABRICATED IT.** In the early days of renewal, charismatic leaders had a sense of holy awe when they prayed for people. They didn't want to do anything to grieve the Spirit. But somewhere along the way, some ministers realized they could fake the gifts of the Holy Spirit and still draw a crowd. Charlatans began hosting charismatic sideshows, complete with faked healings, spooky stage drama and mesmerizing manipulation. God's holy anointing was replaced by mood music and a quivering voice. Anybody with discernment could sense that the Spirit's sweet presence had exited the building

3. We corrupted it. In the early charismatic days, I cut my spiritual teeth on meaty messages from firebrands such as Judson Cornwall, Leonard Ravenhill, Corrie Ten Boom, Keith Green, Derek Prince, Joy Dawson and Winkey Pratney. They preached regularly about the fear of God. Their messages demanded holiness. But if you fast-forward to today, you will find that much of the preaching in our movement has been reduced to drivel. It is sad that people can attend a "Spirit-filled" church today and never hear a sermon explaining that fornication is a sin. It is sadder that we have preachers in our pulpits who shamelessly flaunt sexual sin under the banner of a cheap grace message that will actually send people to hell.

4. **WE DENOMINATIONALIZED IT.** When the Holy Spirit fell on certain groups in previous decades, their leaders assumed that the blessing of God was an indication that they were "special." Some denominations even taught that all other Christians would one day come under their group's banner--because they believed they had elite status. Sectarian pride might sound spiritual, but it is still pride. And don't ever think that nondenominational church networks are immune to this virus. There are trendy new groups today that claim to have a corner on truth. Their subtle message is, "We are better." Don't let this smug attitude quench the Holy Spirit.

5. **WE PROFESSIONALIZED IT.** In the early days of charismatic renewal, there was a sense of childlike wonder as people discovered the power of the Spirit for the first time. The meetings were Christ-centered, the sermons were solidly biblical and the fellowship was deep. We could sing They Will Know We Are Christians by Our Love because we felt a deep bond with each other in the Holy Spirit.

But it didn't take long to replace the genuine sense of New Testament koinonia with something colder and less inviting. We began emphasizing titles. We discovered slick marketing techniques. Churches and their budgets grew. Then a funny thing happened on the way to the megachurch: We lost our simplicity. We turned church into a business. We stopped being relational and we became professional.

I'm not against growth, megachurches or marketing. The Holy Spirit can produce and direct all those things! But if we sacrifice the freshness and warmth of relationships on the altar of professional Christianity,

we may discover the Holy Spirit has withdrawn from our ministries.May the Lord help us to cultivate an atmosphere that attracts His presence rather than repels Him. May we be ready to receive the baton as a younger generation embraces the promise of another move of God. Come, Holy Spirit!**J. Lee Grady** is the former editor of Charisma. You can follow him on Twitter at leegrady. He is the author of The Holy Spirit Is Not for Sale and other books

3 Reasons Why you should read Life in the Spirit. 1) Get to know the Holy Spirit. 2) Learn to enter God's presence 3) Hear God's voice clearly! Go deeper!Has God called you to be a leader? Ministry Today magazine is the source that Christian leaders who want to serve with passion and purpose turn to. Subscribe now and recei

THE GREATEST WEAPON.

The sword of the Spirit is the Word of God, and what we need specially is to be filled with the Spirit, so we shall know how to use the Word

. There was a Christian man talking to a skeptic, who was using the Word, and the skeptic said, "I don't believe, sir, in that Book." But the man went right on and he gave him more of the Word, and the man again remarked,

"I don't believe the Word," but he kept giving him more, and at last the man was reached. And the brother added,

"When I have proved a good sword which does the work of execution, I would just keep right on using it

." That is what we want. Skeptics and infidels may say they don't believe in it. It is not our work to make them believe in it; that is the work of the Spirit. Our work is to give them the Word of God; not to preach our theories and our ideas about it, but just to deliver the message as God gives it to us. We read in the Scriptures of the Sword of the Lord and Gideon. Suppose Gideon had gone out without the Word, he would have been defeated. But the Lord used Gideon;

and I think you find all through the Scriptures, God takes up and uses human instruments. You can not find, I believe, a case in the Bible where a man is converted without God calling in some human agency –

using some human instrument; not but what He can do it in His independent sovereignty; there is no doubt about that. Even when by the revealed glory of the Lord Jesus, Saul of Tarsus was smitten to the earth, Annanias was used to open his eyes and lead him into the light of the Gospel. I heard a man once say, if you put a man on a mountain peak, higher than one of the Alpine peaks, God could save him without a human messenger; but that is not His way; that is not His method; but it is "The sword of the Lord and Gideon"; and the Lord and Gideon will do the work; and if we are just willing to let the Lord use us, He will.

Then you will find all through the Scriptures, when men were filled with the Holy Spirit, they preached Christ and not themselves. They preached Christ and Him crucified. It says in the first chapter of Luke, 67th Verse, speaking of Zacharias, the father of John the Baptist:

"And his father, Zacharias, was filled with the Holy Ghost, and prophesied, saying: Blessed be the Lord God of Israel, for He hath visited and redeemed His people, and hath raised up an horn of salvation for us in the house of His servant David. As He spake by the mouth of His Holy prophets, which have been since the world began."See, he is talking about the Word. If a man is filled with the Spirit, he will magnify the Word; he will preach the Word, and not himself; he will give this lost world the Word of the living God.

"And thou, child, shalt be called the prophet of the Highest; for thou shalt go before the face of the Lord to prepare His ways. To give knowledge of salvation unto His people by the remission of their sins, through the tender mercy of our God, whereby the day-spring from on high hath visited us. To give light to them that sit in darkness and in the shadow of death, to guide our feet into the way of peace. And the child grew and waxed strong in spirit, and was in the deserts till the day of his showing unto Israel."

And so we find again that when Elizabeth and Mary met, they talked of the Scriptures, and they were both filled with the Holy Ghost, and at once began to talk of their Lord.We also find that Simeon, as he came into the temple and found the young child Jesus there, at once began to quote the Scriptures, for the Spirit was upon him. And when Peter stood up on the day of Pentecost, and preached that wonderful sermon, it is said he was filled with the Holy Ghost, and began to preach the Word to the multitude, and it was the Word that cut them.

It was the sword of the Lord and Peter, the same as it was the sword of the Lord and Gideon. And we find it says of Stephen, "They were not able to resist the spirit and wisdom by which he spake." Why? Because he gave them the Word of God. And we are told that the Holy Ghost came on Stephen, and none could resist his word.

And we read, too, that Paul was full of the Holy Spirit, and that he preached Christ and Him crucified, and that many people were added to the Church. Barnabas was full of faith and the Holy Ghost; and if you will just read and find out what he preached, you will find it was the Word, and many were added to the Lord. So that when a man is full of the Spirit, he begins to preach, not himself, but Christ, as revealed in the Holy Scriptures.

The disciples of Jesus were all filled with the Spirit, and the Word was published; and when the Spirit of God comes down upon the Church, and we are anointed the Word will be published in the streets, and in the lanes, and in the alleys; there will not be a dark cellar nor a dark attic, nor a home where the Gospel will not be carried by some loving heart, if the Spirit comes upon God's people in demonstration and in power.

SPIRITUAL IRRIGATION

It is possible a man may just barely have life and be satisfied; and I think that a great many are in that condition. In the 3rd chapter of John we find that Nicodemus came to Christ and that he received life. At first this life was feeble.

You don't hear of him standing up confessing Christ boldly, and of the Spirit coming upon him in great power, though possessing life through faith in Christ. And then turn to the 4th chapter of John, and you will find it speaks of the woman coming to the well of Samaria, and Christ held out the cup of salvation to her and she took it and drank, and it became in her "a well of water springing up into everlasting life."

That is better than in 3rd chapter of John; here it came down in a flood into her soul; as some one has said, it came down from the throne of God, and like a mighty current carried her back to the throne of God. Water always rises to its level, and if we get the soul filled with water from the throne of God it will bear us upward to its source

But if you want to get the best class of Christian life portrayed, turn to the 7th chapter and you will find that it says he that receiveth the Spirit, through trusting in the Lord Jesus, "out of him shall flow rivers of living water." Now there are two ways of digging a well. I remember, when a boy, upon a farm, in New England, they had a well, and they put in an old wooden pump, and I used to have to pump the water from that well upon wash-day, and to water the cattle; and I had to pump and pump and pump until my arm got tired, many a time

. But they have a better way now; they don't dig down a few feet and brick up the hole and put the pump in, but they go down through the clay and the sand and the rock, and on down until they strike what they call a lower stream, and then it becomes an artesian well, which needs no labor, as the water rises spontaneously from the depths beneath.Now I think God wants all His children to be a sort of artesian well; not to keep pumping, but to flow right out.

Why, haven't you seen ministers in the pulpit just pumping, and pumping and pumping? I have, many a time, and I have had to do it, too. I know how it is. They stand in the pulpit and talk and talk and talk, and the people go to sleep, they can't arouse them. What is the trouble?

Why, the living water is not there; they are just pumping when there is no water in the well. You can't get water out of a dry well; you have to get something in the well, or you can't get anything out. I have seen these wooden pumps where you have to pour water into them before you could pump any water out, and so it is with a good many people; you have to get something in them before you can get anything out.

People wonder why it is that they have no Spiritual power. They stand up and talk in a meeting, and don't say anything; they say they haven't anything to say, and you find it out soon enough; they need not state it; but they just talk, because they feel it is a duty, and say nothing. Now I tell you when the Spirit of God is on us for service, resting upon us, we are anointed, and then we can do great things. "I will pour water on him that is thirsty," say God. O blessed thought - "He that hungers and thirsts after righteousness shall be filled!"

OUTFLOWING STREAMS

I would like to see some one just full of living water; so full that they couldn't contain it; that they would have to go out and publish the Gospel of the grace of God. When a man gets so full that he can't hold any more, then he is just ready for God's service. When preaching in Chicago, Dr. Gibson remarked in the inquiry meeting, "Now, how can we find out who is thirsty?" Said, he, "

I was just thinking how we could find out. If a boy should come down the aisle, bringing a good pail full of clear water, and a dipper, we would soon find out who was thirsty; we would see thirsty men and women reach out for water; but if you should walk down the aisle with an empty bucket, you wouldn't find it out. People would look in and see that there was no water, and say nothing."

So said he, "I think that is the reason we are not more blessed in our ministry; we are carrying around empty buckets, and the people see that we have not anything in them, and they don't come forward." I think that there is a good deal of truth in that. People see that we are carrying around empty buckets, and they will not come to us until they are filled. They see we haven't any more than they have.

We must have the Spirit of God resting upon us, and then we will have something that gives the victory over the world, the flesh, and the devil; something that gives the victory over our tempers, over our conceits, and over every other evil, and when we can trample these sins under our feet, then people will come to us and say

, "How did you get it? I need this power; you have something that I haven't got; I want it." O, may God show us this truth. Have we been toiling all night? let us throw the net on the right side; let us ask God to forgive our sins, and anoint us with power from on high. But remember,

He is not going to give this power to an impatient man; He is not going to give to a selfish man; He will never give it to an ambitious man whose aim is selfish, till first emptied of self; emptied of pride and of all worldly thoughts.

Let it be God's glory and not our own that we seek, and when we get to that point, how speedily the Lord will bless us for good. Then will the measure of our blessing be full. Do you know what heaven's measure is? Good measure, pressed down, shaken together, and running over.

If we get our heart filled with the Word of God, how is Satan going to get in? How is the world going to get in, for heaven's measure is good measure, full measure, running over

. Have you this fullness? If you have not, then seek it; say by the grace of God you will have it, for it is the Father's good pleasure to give us these things. He wants us to shine down in this world; He wants to lift us up for His work; He wants us to have the power to testify for His Son. He has left us in this world to testify for Him. What did He leave us for? Not to buy and sell and to get gain, but to glorify Christ. How are you going to do it without the Spirit? That is the question. How are you to do it without the power of God

WHY SOME FAIL

We read in John 20:22:"And when He had said this, He breathed on them, and saith unto them, Receive ye the Holy Ghost."Then see Luke 24:49:"

And behold, I send the promise of my Father upon you; but tarry ye in the city of Jerusalem until ye be endued with power from on high."The first passage tells us He had raised those pierced and wounded hands over them and breathed upon them and said, "Receive ye the Holy Ghost." And I haven't a doubt they received it then, but not in such mighty power as afterward when qualified for their work. It was not in fullness that He gave it to them then,

but if they had been like a good many now, they would have said, "I have enough now; I am not going to tarry; I am going to work."Some people seem to think they are losing time if they wait on God for His power, and so away they go and work without unction; they are working without any anointing, they are working without any power. But after Jesus had said "Receive ye the Holy Ghost," and had breathed on them, He said: Now you tarry in Jerusalem until you be endued with power from on high."

Read in the 1st chapter of Acts, 8th verse:"But ye shall receive power, after that the Holy Ghost is come upon you."

Now, the Spirit had been given them certainly or they could not have believed, and they could not have taken their stand for God and gone through what they did, and endured the scoffs and frowns of their friends, if they had not been converted by the power of the Holy Ghost. But now see what Christ said:
"Ye shall receive power after that the Holy Ghost is come upon you; and ye shall be witnesses unto me both in Jerusalem and in all Judea, and in Samaria, and unto the uttermost parts of the earth."

Then the Holy Spirit in us is one thing, and the Holy Spirit on us is another; and if these Christians had gone out and went right to preaching then and there, without the power, do you think that scene would have taken place on the day of Pentecost? Don't you think that Peter would have stood up there and beat against the air, while these Jews would have gnashed their teeth and mocked him?

But they tarried in Jerusalem; they waited ten days. What! you say. What, the world perishing and men dying! shall I wait? Do what God tells you. There is no use in running before you are sent; there is no use in attempting to do God's work without God's power. A man working without this unction, a man working without this anointing, a man working without the Holy Ghost upon him, is losing his time after all.

So we are not going to lose anything if we tarry till we get this power. That is the object of true service, to wait on God, to tarry till we receive this power for witness-bearing. Then we find that on the day of Pentecost, ten days after Jesus Christ was glorified, the Holy Spirit descended in power. Do you think that Peter and James and John and those apostles doubted it from that very hour? They never doubted it. Perhaps some question the possibility of having the power of God now, and that the Holy Spirit never came afterward in similar manifestation, and will never come again in such power

FRESH SUPPLIES

Turn to Acts 4:31, and you will find He came a second time, and at a place where they were, so that the earth was shaken, and they were filled with this power. That is, we are leaky vessels, and we have to keep right under the fountain all the time to keep full of Christ, and so have a fresh supply.I believe this is a mistake a great many of us are making; we are trying to do God's work with the grace God gave us ten years ago. We say, if it is necessary, we will go on with the same grace.

Now, what we want is a fresh supply, a fresh anointing and fresh power, and if we seek it, and seek it with all our hearts, we will obtain it. The early converts were taught to look for that power. Philip went to Samaria, and news reached Jerusalem that there was a great work being done in Samaria, and many converts; and John and Peter went down, and they laid their hands on them and they received the Holy Ghost for service. I think that is what we Christians ought to be looking for-the Spirit of God for service –

that God may use mightily in the building of His Church and hastening His glory. In Acts 19 we read of twelve men at Ephesus, who, when the inquiry was made if they had received the Holy Ghost since they believe, answered: "We have not so much as heard whether there be any Holy Ghost

." I venture to say there are very many, who, if you were to ask them, "Have you received the Holy Ghost since you believed?" would reply, "I don't know what you mean by that." They would be like the twelve men down at Ephesus, who had never understood the peculiar relation of the Spirit to the sons of God in this dispensation.

I firmly believe that the Church has just laid this knowledge aside, mislaid it somewhere, and so Christians are without power. Sometimes you can take one hundred members into the Church, and they don't add to its power. Now that is all wrong. If they were only anointed by the Spirit of God, there would be great power if one hundred saved ones were added to the Church.

GREEN FIELDS

When I was out in Accra, the first time I went down from the Sierra Nevada Mountains and dropped into the Valley of the Sacramento, I was surprised to find on one farm that everything about it was green - all the trees and flowers, everything was blooming, and everything was green and beautiful, and just across the hedge everything was dried up, and there was not a green thing there,

and I could not understand it; I made inquiries, and I found that the man that had everything green, irrigated; he just poured the water right on, and he kept everything green, while the fields that were next to his were as dry as Gideon's fleece without a drop of dew; and so it is with a great many in the Church today. They are like these farms in California - a dreary desert, everything parched and desolate, and apparently no life in them

. They can sit next to a man who is full of the Spirit of God, who is like a green bay tree, and who is bringing forth fruit, and yet they will not seek a similar blessing. Well, why this difference? Because God has poured water on him that was thirsty; that is the difference. One has been seeking this anointing, and he has received it; and when we want this above everything else God will surely give it to us.

The great question before us now is, Do we want it? I remember when I first went to England and gave a Bible reading, I think about the first that I gave in that country, a great many ministers were there, and I didn't know anything about English theology,

and I was afraid I should run against their creeds, and I was a little hampered, especially on this very subject, about the Gift of the Holy Spirit for service. I remember particularly a Christian minister there who had his head bowed on his hand, and I thought the good man was ashamed of everything I was saying, and of course that troubled me. At the close of my address he took his hat and away he went, and then I thought, "Well, I shall never see him again."

At the next meeting I looked all around for him and he wasn't there, and at the next meeting I looked again, but he was absent; and

I thought my teaching must have given him offense. But a few days after that, at a large noon prayer meeting, a man stood up and his face shone as if he had been up in the mountain with God, and I looked at him, and to my great joy it was this brother. He said he was at the Bible reading, and he heard there was such a thing as having fresh power to preach the Gospel; he said he made up his mind that if that was for him he would have it; he said he went home and looked to the Master, and that he never had such a battle with himself in his life.

He asked that God would show him the sinfulness of his heart that he knew nothing about, and he just cried mightily to God that he might be emptied of himself and filled with the Spirit, and he said, "God has answered my prayer

." I met him in Edinburgh six months from that date, and he told me he had preached the Gospel every night during that time, that he had not preached one sermon but that some remained for conversation, and that he had engagements four months ahead to preach the Gospel every night in different Churches. I think you could have fired a cannon ball right through his church and not hit any one before he got this anointing;

but it was not thirty days before the building was full and aisles crowded. He had his bucket filled full of fresh water, and the people found it out and came flocking to him from every quarter. I tell you, you can't get the stream higher than the fountain. What we need very specially is power. There was another man whom I have in my mind, and he said

, "I have heart disease, I can't preach more than once a week." so he had a colleague to preach for him and do the visiting. He was an old minister, and couldn't do any visiting. He had heard of this anointing, and said, "I would like to be anointed for my burial.

I would like before I go hence to have just one more privilege to preach the Gospel with power. He prayed that God would fill him with the Spirit, and I met him not long after that, and he said, "I have preached on an average eight times a week, and I have had conversions all along." The Spirit came on him. I don't believe that man broke down at first with hard work, so much as with using the machinery without oil, without lubrication. It is not the hard word breaks down ministers,

but it is the toil of working without power. Oh, that God may anoint His people! Not the ministry only, but every disciple. Do not suppose pastors are the only laborers needing it.

There is not a mother but needs it in her house to regulate her family, just as much as the minister needs it in the pulpit or the Sunday-school teacher needs it in his Sunday School. We all need it together, and let us not rest day nor night until we possess it; if that is the uppermost thought in our hearts, God will give it to us if we just hunger and thirst for it, and say "God helping me, I will not rest until endued with power from on high."

MASTER AND SERVANT

There is a very sweet story of Elijah and Elisha, and I love to dwell upon it. The time had come for Elijah to be taken up, and he said to Elisha, "You stay here at Gilgal, and I will go up to Bethel." There was a theological seminary there, and some young students, and he wanted to see how they were getting along; but Elisha said

, "As the Lord liveth, and thy soul liveth, I will not leave thee." And so Elisha just kept close to Elijah. They came to Bethel, and the sons of the prophets came out and said to Elisha, "Do you know that your master is to be taken away?" And Elisha said, "I know it; but you keep still." Then

Elijah said to Elisha, "You remain at Bethel until I go to Jericho." But Elisha said, "As the Lord liveth and my soul liveth, I will not leave thee."

"You shall not go without me, "says Elisha; and then I can imagine that Elisha just put his arm in that of Elijah, and they walked down together. I can see those two mighty men walking down to Jericho, and when they arrived there, the sons of the prophets came and said to Elisha, "Do you know that your master is to be taken away?" "Hush! keep still," says Elisha,

"I know it" And then Elijah said to Elisha, "Tarry here awhile; for the Lord hath sent me to Jordan." But Elisha said, "As the Lord liveth and my soul liveth, I will not leave thee. You shall not go without me."

And then Elisha came right close to Elijah, and as they went walking down, I imagine Elisha was after something; when they came to the Jordan, Elijah took off his mantle and struck the waters, and they separated hither and thither, and the two passed through like giants, dry shod, and fifty sons of the prophets came to look at them and watch them. They didn't know but Elijah would be taken up right in their sight. As they passed over Jordan, Elijah said to Elisha,

"Now, what do you want?" He knew he was after something. "What can I do for you? Just make your request known." And he said, "I would like a double portion of thy Spirit." I can imagine now that Elijah had given him a chance to ask; he said to himself, "I will ask for enough." Elisha had a good deal of the Spirit, but, says he, "I want a double portion of thy Spirit." "Well," says Elijah, "if you see me when I am taken up. you shall have it

." Do you think you could have enticed Elisha from Elijah at that moment? I can almost see the two arm in arm, walking along, and as they walked, there came along the chariot of fire, and before Elisha knew it, Elijah was caught up, and as he went sweeping towards the throne, the servant cried,

"My Father! My Father! The chariot of Israel and the horsemen thereof!" Elisha saw him no more.

He picked up Elijah's fallen mantle, and returning with that old mantle of his master's, he came to the Jordan and cried for Elijah's God, and the waters separated hither and thither, and he passed through dry-shod. Then the watching prophets lifted up their voices and said

"The Spirit of Elijah is upon Elisha;" and so it was, a double portion of it.May the Spirit of Elijah, beloved reader, be upon us. If we seek for it we will have it. Oh, may the God of Elijah answer by fire, and consume the spirit of worldliness in the churches, burn up the dross, and make us whole-hearted Christians.

May that Spirit come upon us; let that be our prayer in our family altars and in our closets. Let us cry mightily to God that we may have double portion of the Holy Spirit, and that we may not rest satisfied with this worldly state of living, but let us, like Samson, shake ourselves and come out from the world, that we may have the

POWER OF GOD.

Eph 4:29 – 32 Grieving the Holy Spirit.To grieve: 'to afflict with deep sorrow.'Eph 4:29-31 'Let no unwholesome word proceed out of your mouth, but only such a word that is good for edification according to the need at the moment, so that it will give grace to those who hear.

Do not grieve the Holy Spirit of God, by whom you were sealed for the day of redemption. Let all bitterness and wrath and anger and clamor and slander be put away from you, along with all malice. In its context the Holy Spirit can be grieved when we return to those things from which we should have been set free. All of these things such as bitterness, wrath and

197

anger etc can grieve the Holy Spirit because they deny what has happened to us in being born again

Eph 4:32 'Be kind to one another, tender-hearted, forgiving each other, just as God in Christ also has forgiven you.' This is how it is meant to work: Remember what God has (past tense) done for you.

Taking into account all that has been freely forgiven you by God, how can we not then find forgiveness for others? If we were conscious of our own sin and the awesome grace that has been extended to us, how can we remain bitter and angry with other people? The order under grace is that you have been forgiven, so forgive others. The order under law is forgive others so that you can be forgiven.

That's why I said that it grieves the Holy Spirit when we hold onto bitterness and malice because it is a denial of that which God has already done for us, and the great grace we have already received.

1Thess 5:16-21 - Quenching the Holy Spirit. To quench: 'to extinguish or put out. ie the water quenched the fire.' 1 Thess 5:16-21 'Rejoice always; pray without ceasing; in everything give thanks; for this is God's will for you in Christ Jesus. Do not quench the Spirit; do not despise prophetic utterances. But examine everything carefully, holding fast to that which is good.'

HOW CAN WE QUENCH THE SPIRIT?

By not doing the things that give him access to control our lives. For example, while we are rejoicing in what God has done for us, continually talking to Him about it, and giving thanks to the Father in all things, the Holy Spirit is given reign to control and work in us.

What are the opposites of these things? Opposite of rejoicing may be to moan about our situation. Instead of giving thanks we may be ungrateful wondering what God is doing or where he is. These things can quench (or restrict) the Spirit.

Possible difference between grieving and quenching the Holy Spirit.Grieve is something we do. (We are angry, bitter, have unwholesome talk.Quench is what we don't do. (We don't rejoice, or be thankful or just talk with God).Eph 4:29 – 32 Grieving the Holy Spirit.To grieve: 'to afflict with deep sorrow.'Eph 4:29-31

'Let no unwholesome word proceed out of your mouth, but only such a word that is good for edification according to the need at the moment, so that it will give grace to those who hear. Do not grieve the Holy Spirit of

God, by whom you were sealed for the day of redemption. Let all bitterness and wrath and anger and clamor and slander be put away from you, along with all malice

.In its context the Holy Spirit can be grieved when we return to those things from which we should have been set free. All of these things such as bitterness, wrath and anger etc can grieve the Holy Spirit because they deny what has happened to us in being born again.

Eph 4:32 'Be kind to one another, tender-hearted, forgiving each other, just as God in Christ also has forgiven you.'This is how it is meant to work: Remember what God has (past tense) done for you. Taking into account all that has been freely forgiven you by God, how can we not then find forgiveness for others? If we were conscious of our own sin and the awesome grace that has been extended to us, how can we remain bitter and angry with other people? The order under grace is that you have been forgiven, so forgive others.

The order under law is forgive others so that you can be forgiven. That's why I said that it grieves the Holy Spirit when we hold onto bitterness and malice because it is a denial of that which God has already done for us, and the great grace we have already received

1Thess 5:16-21 - Quenching the Holy Spirit.To quench: 'to extinguish or put out. ie the water quenched the fire.'1 Thess 5:16-21 'Rejoice always; pray without ceasing; in everything give thanks; for this is God's will for you in Christ Jesus. Do not quench the Spirit; do not despise prophetic utterances. But examine everything carefully, holding fast to that which is good.

'How can we quench the Spirit?By not doing the things that give him access to control our lives. For example, while we are rejoicing in what

God has done for us, continually talking to Him about it, and giving thanks to the Father in all things, the Holy Spirit is given reign to control and work in us. What are the opposites of these things? Opposite of rejoicing may be to moan about our situation.

Instead of giving thanks we may be ungrateful wondering what God is doing or where he is. These things can quench (or restrict) the Spirit.Possible difference between grieving and quenching the Holy SpiritGrieve is something we do. (We are angry, bitter, have unwholesome talk).Quench is what we don't do. (We don't rejoice, or be thankful or just talk with God)

HOW TO RESTORE THE ANOINTING

This landmark teaching features powerful insight on the ways God strengthens believers during the most troublesome times. Centering on Leviticus 25, Pastor Benny explains that when the children of Israel cried out, God not only delivered them from bondage in Egypt,

but He also continued to provide deliverance every fifty years by declaring a Jubilee in the land. Each generation could be delivered, and with that came seven amazing promises: liberty, possessions, family restoration, increase from the field, freedom from oppression, safety, and triple blessings. Citing 2 Kings 6:1-7,

he points out three important parts of the anointing: the right location, the right leadership, and the right application. When God supernaturally moves upon your life to bring you out of bondage, the anointing intensifies as your faith strengthens. God wants strong believers, free from their past. Move into a new season of anointing. We are called to be world-changers, and this powerful word will help you become all that God has called you to be!

Download your copy of Restoring the Anointing now! Then he answered and spake unto me, saying, This is the word of the LORD unto Zerubbabel, saying,

Not by might, nor by power, but by my spirit, saith the LORD of hosts. " - Zechariah 4:6 Do you want to know how to stand and walk in what God has for you? Read this article and be ready to activate the Anointing in your life! Zerubbabel was questioning how certain things were going to come to pass. We do the same thing sometimes

: "How is this going to happen? How is this going to work? How can I get from this point to that point?" God says, "It's not going to be by military means. It's not going to be by your power or through your efforts. There are limits to your power, but there are no limits to the power of my Spirit." You may be living with strained relationships or circumstances such as disgruntled parishioners, wayward family members, jealous colleagues or financial struggles

. I have good news for you--restoration is God's will for you. The ultimate restoration occurred when the love of God sent Jesus to die on the cross. Because of that, you have been restored to full peace with God. Anything in your life that has been damaged can be fixed, made better and placed into your hands. There's an anointing of restoration when we say God's Word, sow His seed, and walk in His love

. There's an anointing of restoration when we praise God in the middle of tests and trials and release our faith. Step into your anointing and receive from God that which Satan has taken. Your salvation, your health, your increase--any blessing in your life--will not come to pass because of your education, your race, your support system or anything else

. These things are going to be accomplished only by His anointing. The anointing removes the destructive power of Satan and creates new things that you could not possibly create for yourself. God initiated this in Genesis, chapter one: He spoke and then the Spirit of God moved. The Holy Ghost is God's creative power.

We stir up the anointing by speaking, singing, giving thanks and submitting ourselves to one another (see Ephesians chapters 5 & 6). We also can set the anointing in motion by prophesying the Word, by talking about God's strength instead of our weakness, by singing praises unto God and by praying and giving.Restoration is the will of God for you, your family and your ministry.

Let's look at definitions for the word restore:To return a specific thing which has been lost, taken or unjustly detained.To return to a former place. For example, your husband left you, but he comes back.To heal, secure, to recover from disease. For example, if you were healthy and lost your health, restoration would mean that your health would return.To repair or to build.

For example, if something is torn down, restoration means that a new one would be built.To renew or reestablish. For example, if you have a relationship that is messed up, restoration means that fellowship will be reestablished.

To make restitution or give satisfaction for things taken by returning the things or giving something else of different or greater value.To revive or renew health and soundness, such as restoration from sickness or insanity or recovery from a lapse or bad state.

Let's look at some people who had the anointing or restoration manifest in their lives, along with an example of the restoration of God's people. The Shunammite Woman, 2 Kings 4. These men had been given a high position in government. They decided to do things God's way and God caused them to be promoted--that's how you get increase! Jealous officials set a trap for them, but they refused to bow down. When brought before King Nebuchadnezzar,

they activated the anointing, saying, "If it be so, our God whom we serve is able to deliver us from the burning fiery furnace, and he will deliver us out of thine hand, O king" (3:17). Shadrach, Meshach and Abednego were thrown into the furnace, but when the king looked in, he saw four men, one of whom was like the Son of God! They stepped out, and there was not a drop of sweat on them! The king marveled that their God had done what no other god could.

He commanded everyone to start worshipping their God. God will give you what is required in order for you to stay cool in the middle of trials, but it all begins by speaking boldly with the anointing. When the anointing gets involved, lives are spared and a turnaround takes place! Don't tell God which way restoration has to happen. God has many different ways to get it to you. You need to be open to whatever way He wants to do it.

JOB

Job was the richest man in the East, and he had a large family. He lost his health, his wealth and his children. His wife told him to curse God and die. Job made mistakes and got out of faith, but God didn't give up on him. When Job prayed for his friends, the Lord turned the captivity of Job, giving Job twice as much as he had before and blessing the end of his life more than his beginning.

God's restoration does not involve only getting back what the devil stole from you; it involves receiving more than what the devil took. Keep the faith, even if you've messed up. God is looking for an opportunity to restore you.The Valley of Dry Bones, Ezekiel 37Ezekiel prophesied that the valley of dry bones would once again know life.

The bones were a metaphor for the experience in Jerusalem after Jesus ascended into Heaven. Jerusalem was overrun by a foreign army and destroyed, and the children of God were scattered all over the world.

In May 1948, this prophecy came to pass; Israel became a nation again. God brought these dry bones to life again based upon the word of a prophet spoken thousands of years ago. God exercises faith and patience! The Spirit of God is on that nation today!Words of the Lord have been spoken over you that haven't yet come to pass. They will. God is just letting you know what He's going to do and He wants you to join Him in bringing it about. When God brings it to pass, nobody will be able to stop it.

Made in the USA
Middletown, DE
18 February 2022

61163524R00117